# ECHOES
## *Her Journey to Grace*

# ECHOES
## Her Journey to Grace

## Written by
## Billie R. S. Shouse

*BRS Ministries*
*2020*

I AM Productions, LLC Publishing
*Est. 2003*

Printed and bound in the United States of America
First Printing: 2020

ISBN: 978-1-7923-0590-0

Editing by Teresa A. Moore
Published by I AM Productions, LLC
Davenport, IA 52807
www.iamproductionsllc.com
iamproductions2003@yahoo.com

Cover Art and Graphic Design by Gwen Ballard Patton (ballardpatton@outlook.com). All rights reserved. Cover art may not be reproduced or used in any manner whatsoever without the express written permission of the artist.

# *Table of Contents*

## *This Book is dedicated to*
## *All of the Beautiful Ladies*

*Mothers, Sisters, Daughters, Granddaughters, and Friends that I have encountered throughout my life. You have all added a significant part to the puzzle that I call the "female experience". My desire is to inspire you to laugh with me, cry with me, and to reflect, as the facts unfold. We all share together every hope and dream that calls us beautiful. Fearfully and wonderfully made by God.*

### *Special Recognition*

*To my dear Mother, you are the wind beneath the wings of my heart.*

*My special acknowledgement and thank you to my editor, Teresa, who has worked diligently on my behalf in each of my projects. We have persevered, never forgetting the days of "dressing and bread". (Only she will understand) She is a confidant, a friend and the greatest Sister. Your honesty and passion for me, even if we didn't agree on our strategy, has been my fuel.*

*Thank you, Julie. Watching your tenacity and resilience even in the face of dilemma gives me courage. You inspire me even when you think I'm not watching.*

*To my sister Juanita, you are the reflection that keeps me looking in the mirror.*

*I love you all dearly and thank you from my heart for your support and your PUSH, that gives me courage to dig deeper and have the tenacity to reach for the stars.*

*Finally, Shauna, Shannon, Sharee, Ila, Billie, Neveah, and Ileah, my personal "sisterhood", you give me life.*

*Billie*

# *The Beauty of a Woman*

*The beauty of a woman is not in the clothes she wears,*
*The figure that she carries,*
*Or the way she combs her hair.*

*The beauty of a woman must be seen from in her eyes,*
*Because that is the doorway to her heart,*
*The place where love resides.*

*The beauty of a woman is not in a facial mole,*
*But true beauty in a woman,*
*Is reflected in her soul.*

*It is the caring that she lovingly gives,*
*The passion that she shows.*
*And the beauty of a woman*
*With passing years, only grows.*

*By Audrey Hepburn*

# *JOURNEY PREFACE*

UGLY!!

FAT GIRL!!

YOU LOOK LIKE YOU'VE GAINED WEIGHT!!

YOU LOOK ANEREXIC ---- SKINNY --- FLAT CHEST!

IS THAT A MUSTACHE?

YOU LOOK LIKE A BOY!!

HE CAN'T STAND YOU!!  HE LIKES HER.

SHES PRETTIER THAN YOU!!

AND, WHAT IN THE WORLD MAKES YOU THINK THEY

WOULD CHOOSE YOU?

BIG NOSE --- NAPPY HEAD --- WHY DON'T YOU GET

SOME NEW CLOTHES?

DARKIE --- HONKIE---BEANER

HIGH YELLOW!! --- WHITE TRASH!! ---BEANER!!!

STUCK UP!!

YOU THINK YOU CUTE!!

DUMMY!!

NO. SORRY, YOU AIN'T SMART ENOUGH TO DO THAT

YOUR HAIR WON'T EVEN MOVE.

IS THAT YOUR REAL HAIR?

YOUR WET HAIR SMELLS LIKE A DOG!!

BIG LIPS! BIG MOUTH! GET YOUR TEETH FIXED!!

YOU GOT SOME BIG FEET!!

!!!!!!!!!!!!!!!!!!!!!!!!!!!!!!!!!!!!!!!!!!!!!!!!!!!!!!!!!!!!!!!!!!!!!!!!!!!!!!!!!!!!!

Please excuse the broken English displayed in portions of the words above. Sometimes, it is necessary to do so to drive a very needed point into our psyche. These words and even uglier ones have stabbed women in the back and caused them to retreat into corners and tremble in fear as they respond to the judgement of a cruel world. I myself, and the Sisterhood that I am striving to affect, have personally been on the receiving end of many of these devastating words.

As a child, I struggled with the idea of beauty simply because my hair did not easily flow in the wind. Though the braids hung long and thick like a heavy rope, it was not considered acceptable beauty. It was not 'good hair'.

After all of the exhausting work that my mother did to make me feel better, unbraiding, straightening, and allowing my hair to flow down my back, the next step of the abuse was even worse. Jealous rages spewed out of the mouths of little girls who felt that somehow this new hairstyle gave me some sort of prestige. What hurt so deeply was the fact that most of the little girls that dosed out this hatred were ones who looked just like me. They did not understand that I was just like them, facing every insecurity, with the hope of not being left behind in the critical judgement of myself.

Forced into an unexpected and new playground of competition, a defeated spirit took residence, pushing me into a lifetime of allowing others to decide the definition of my beauty.

That was then!! Now, I must respond to those opinions with a huge 'no thank you!!' That, in itself is not an easy task. With each new fad and the dawn of the next month, the struggle continues. I must reassure myself, whether the day is good or bad, that I decide who I am.

Until you come to terms with your own strengths and weaknesses, and are comfortable with your own solutions, you will never be convinced of how beautiful you really are. You will spend a lifetime in a misery that refuses to give you permission to survive.

Many do not understand my resolve to not get stuck in a definition that only coincides with the current fad. No one person or designer should have the power to force upon society their particular code of what is acceptable for everyone. No comedian should be applauded and accepted as they tear down and destroy a woman's beauty just to get a laugh. And we as women, **must** have strength enough to determine what we want, and to not be the victims of the latest fashions and causes that fade as quickly as they come. We must not be the carriers of hatred, jealousy, and backstabbing agendas that further sanction our demise, and divide us as women. These mentalities only promote a system that annihilates the very spirit of embracing and celebrating our individual beauty. The new goal must be to no longer depend upon the approval of men, but to understand that God has fearfully and wonderfully formed us. Accepting this much needed change will finally start the process of a long overdue healing.

Every unfair, biased, and mishandled situation judged by men, that we have encountered throughout history, as we unfold the 'female experience', were managed totally different by Jesus Christ.

He never sees women as inferior but gives her His equal 'grace'. He has pulled the worst out of horrific circumstances and honored them as important and significant. He allowed many restored women who were rejected by society, as He walked the earth, to surround and support His Scriptural Kingdom assignment to touch the lost.

Even behind her greatest failure, God made a way of escape for her. She was not excused, but she was forgiven, not abolished, but given a destiny.

Men hold the sin of Eve against her still, placing all women in an inferior state. But God has redeemed her by His blood and put her back in her glorious position of honor and grace. And no man can pluck her out. Deal with it!!

CONSIDER: If God restored Adam, who was created in the image of God and yet **he** failed, and the world still reveres him with kingly status, what would make you think that God would be so cruel to leave Eve without hope? It does not compute!

My dear Sisters, I invite you to walk with me on this journey of discovery into our femininity as we divulge sensitive information and attempt to start to break the barriers that have too long been set up for our destruction. A destruction that unfairly has labeled our gender throughout the generations. I open these corridors and release the hinges of truth. Though many have attempted to silence every cry of unfair pain, every broken promise, and every sound that demands accountability, I set them free… Please join me, my Sisters as we experience.

## *"ECHOES"*
### *Her Journey of Grace*

# INTRODUCTION PART 1:

## What Is Beauty?

In today's society, more time and money have been spent on beauty and physical appearance than any other time in history. The millennial motto appears to be, "Look good, feel good". According to a July 2017 study by Groupon, The New York Post, revealed that American women will spend nearly a quarter of a million dollars on their appearance in their lifetime. That averages out to be $313.00 a month, $3,756.00 a year, and $225,360.00 over a lifetime, for women ages 18 to78. Men are not far behind, spending, $221.00 a month and $175,680.00 over their lifetime. The study further states that over one-third of women say they would consider plastic surgery to obtain a more youthful look.

The lines of definition of what is considered attractive or not have changed considerably. Society has demanded that individuals be allotted the privilege of defining for themselves what they view as beautiful. But even though these lines have stretched considerably, the undertones of a skeptical world still force the thinking of many to be tainted to embody biased views and force the mind to retreat in obscurity when one feels unaccepted.

The unspeakable negative effect that this way of thinking has placed on our youth have forced the abusive hands of those who have made it their mission to be oppressors. Anyone who feels inferior to what is deemed as 'popular' and 'in', teeters on the grace of the intimidator to survive. Incapable of sustaining the pressure of these bullies, many have succumbed to all sorts of atrocities which often result in them committing suicide.

We speak, 'be yourself', but constantly experience the results of criticism expressed by a judgmental glance if our appearance falls outside of the status quo. So, in reality, what has beauty really given in return besides creating either prejudice or pleasure only for the one who finds it to their liking? Thus, we hear the expression that, 'it is in the eyes of the beholder'. This statement solidifies the fact that there is no set definition for beauty. Some of the most attractive people to look at have portrayed the most repulsive personalities, while some considered less beautiful have the most charismatic persona.

So, I would ask, what is beauty? Scripture defines it as vain or vanity (*Proverbs 31*). Biblical definition eludes to this meaning; something resulting out of pride that is ultimately inconsequential. In other words, with or without the physical appearance of beauty, God's judgement of what you do is more important than how you look. He desires that we finally realize that to Him, it is the beauty of proper motive and effective lifestyle that pleasures Him most. Thank you, Lord!

If we were actually judged by God for the size of our dress, the texture of our hair, the tone of our skin, or for our ability to mesmerize everyone we encounter, then what in the world could we possibly need from Him? His ability to make us the attractive vessels He has established in His plans for us, is more important than any blush, lip gloss, or eyeliner you can purchase at the local cosmetic counter. It is healthier than any level your physical trainer can take you to, and it is more enduring than a shot of Botox. The same God who has fearfully and wonderfully made us, in His image, is the same One who is more than capable of presenting us faultless (or may I say flawless) before the presence of His glory WITH EXCEEDING JOY!! His love changes the mindset and allows us to not only diagnose the 'Female Experience', but puts into perspective, spiritually and Biblically, not just the beauty that seems to be at the forefront, but more importantly, her glory and her grace.

These beautiful, complicated, creatures have been misunderstood and misdiagnosed for centuries. And anytime that something is observed without understanding, it is left open to be mishandled.

Women have been pushed to not only be degraded, but to believe and grasp the degradation themselves. In each culture, you see women treated as lower classed citizens, destined to be the victims of the perversions of men. Many women are so desperate to be seen as beautiful and desirable, that they are reduced to insane measures to accomplish the goal. Here are just a few examples from the article, *Bizarre Beauty Rituals from Around the World,* provided by *World press; the clever.com*; and *slice.ca,* that I found while researching this subject.

Eastern cultures bind the feet of women in an effort to keep the feet small. This mutilation begins between the ages of 4-7. All of the young girls' toes are broken with the exception of the largest toe. They are then wrapped with binding cloth so that they will not grow to normal size. This act is done to make a young woman more desirable for marriage than for a working career.

Young girls in Sumatra must go through a beauty treatment known as "teeth chiseling". The local shaman sharpens a rude blade as best he can and takes a rock and starts to hack away, without any deadening whatsoever. This is said to make her more attractive to men. She, unfortunately, has no say in the matter at all.

The young women of Thailand start at approximately age 5, placing rings around their necks, adding more as they age. These long giraffe-like necks are said to be beautiful and necessary to attract men. They suffer a lifetime of restricted movement because long necks are the standard for beauty despite the pain.

In Nigeria and South Africa, large hot stones, hammers, or spatulas are burned over hot coals and pressed against the breasts of young girls to kill breast tissue and stunt growth. The goal is to make the girls less sexually attractive to boys and men and to guard them from rape. My question; *"What about the men?"*

I could continue by speaking of genital mutilation in Uganda, Somalia, India and Pakistan, and the nude street beatings in Brazil, just to touch the surface of the torture's women receive in order to please men.

The women of Mauritania are force fed, because a plump woman makes a husband appear prosperous. Held in prison camps, they are forced to eat 16,000 calories a day and beaten if they cannot hold the food down. All to fit a paradigm of supposed beauty to make them desirable for marriage. This insanity further diminishes the character of U.S. women on the other end of the spectrum, when they allow their bodies to be injected with foreign chemicals to produce big butts, only to end up in a filthy music video. False beauty, minimized to gyrations and filthy acts that push them even further into humiliation, and still not seen as precious and beautiful. What further causes me to shudder is the fact that most of these rituals are demanded by men and carried out by other women, because, THEY HAVE NO VOICE!! Women who have attempted to stand up and be strong in the fight for change and to raise their voices against some of these rituals, pay a price for the retaliation that is both brutal and unprecedented.

I recently watched the 2011 Oscar winning documentary called "*Saving Face*". I cringed at the cases of women in the Pakistan culture whose husbands, if they got angry, threw acid on their wives to intentionally disfigure and maim them. In one of the worse cases, the family of the husband participated in the crime. The husband is said to have poured acid on his wife, the father-in-law then threw gas on her, and finally, the mother-in-law threw fire and they locked her in a room to burn, with her children on the other side of the wall. She somehow survived. It took years of struggle and litigation for their government to finally write laws of punishment against such crimes. Yes, in other words, they were getting away without punishment until a group of women lawyers fought to bring justice to these brutalized women. Men have long been justified in treating women like lower classed citizens, put on earth to be controlled and owned like property, instead of handling them like the beautiful creatures they were created to be. If you are not convinced, go on the internet and look at cases of women being brutalized in every culture. Many of these cases are posted online like movies. My question. Who are the individuals who stand laughing and recording such behavior without reaching out to help? You have become just as guilty!!

It is important to understand that God has never and will never sanction this behavior. There will be a day of reckoning! When? It is in His hands to know the days and the times.

Though man thinks one way, God does not withhold the good from us when we desire to be in His will. That is why it is necessary for us to understand that until we denounce from our psyche every curse of the past that exists based on our physical presentation, we will be locked under the bondage of men forever. We must pray that in cultures where women lack the freedom of choice, deliverance will finally come. However, those who can choose their own fate, must empower one another to embrace our choices with wisdom.

Have my bad experiences caused me to question my value and affected my life? ABSOLUTELY!! But if you are not ready to move forward with a new perspective, you will be buried in bitterness and pain. It is time, my Sisters, to see your beauty through the eyes of God and not of man.

When God created Woman and presented her to man, she was the greatest gift ever given. As perfect as man was, being in the image and purpose of God, the woman was fashioned and perfectly constructed as the specified vessel to give glory to Adam. She was a part of him, and she had dominion and ruled Eden *with* him. She was DESIGNED and FASHONED for that Glory. She was fitly joined together and was a designers' dream. Her arms were perfect, her bustline contoured the body into perfection, the waistline measured exact for Adam's arms, and her hips and legs finished the design to Adam's delight. She was a masterpiece, fashioned by the Master, the greatest designer of all time. And as beautiful and desirable as she was to Adam, she was even more precious to God.

However, listening to the wrong voice and desiring to be wise, pushed Woman to lose her glory and require grace. Sin caused this perfect design of righteousness to resist her original design and have to be reconstructed for another purpose. Though created perfectly, her shoulders shrank, her breast line drooped, her waist bulged, and her hips expanded. Leaving her in the position to be judged by her appearance, instead of the glory she once walked in as a partner and not a servant. Even today, women work hard to maintain what was given to Eve without toil. So, the only way that the designer could reevaluate His design was to change her glory into grace and tailor a way for every woman in the future to be able to fit His design.

So, now her glory requires <u>His</u> grace!

The marred vessel must be refashioned to fit a new design. And so, the Master tailor goes to work. He suffers a thorn here, and a nail there, a stripe down the back and side, a slap here and a little spit there, look closely and you will see some blood and sweat and a splash of water to cleanse the fabric and get the stains out. RE-ASSEMBLED, though the first glory is gone, He MAKES IT ANOTHER VESSEL fit for the Masters' use and tailored for his purpose.

So, God takes what has been marred, and abused, and misused, and makes it over again! It does not matter to God how far the 'glory' has departed; though the glory be tainted, I will tailor it by my grace!!! I will redesign a beautiful vessel that now exists for *My* glory!!

Part of the beauty of who we are as women is the fact that we are capable of giving and taking so much. This trait often causes us to lose sight of our value. We give to everything and everyone around us and it seems, in return, that everything is snatched from us. We hurt over all sorts of losses that rob us of who God intended for us to be. That is why the Master, the same creator of the Glory, is the only one who can shield us from all of the 'mess' and bring us into the presence of His Grace.

When we are marred, we allow others to come in and further stain us. We allow men to treat us any kind of way because we feel that is all we deserve. Women who have been raped often experience their glory being shifted to a hatred of what they were created for. They somehow feel that both their nature and character have been compromised and destroyed. The beauty of their love then changes to distortion.

Dreadful experiences refuse to allow the love of God to reconstruct us, so, we surrender to alcohol, drugs, or promiscuity. Behind this, hopelessness. But my dear sister's God has come to give you an *ABUNDANT LIFE*! That life releases you from the past and prepares you for a better future.

Only God can restore and resurrect what is dead. Every shattered dream, every broken possibility. So many of us have either given up or had the glory stolen from us so long ago that we don't even remember what that beauty ever felt or looked like.

Oprah Winfrey said it like this in *The Color Purple*; "I know what it is to want to sing and have it beat out of you." Things can be Beat out, resulting in bruises and broken bones. They can be Spoken out, by words that destroy character. They can be Touched out, by foreign incestuous or molesting hands of abuse. But I declare that no matter how you suffered this loss, that the beauty shall replace the ashes. Because the TAILOR OF GRACE, has promised:

*... to give unto them Beauty for Ashes, the oil of joy for mourning, the garment of praise for the spirit of heaviness... (Isaiah 61:3 NKJV)*

Your beauty, restored by, His Grace. No matter what obstacles you face that attempt to destroy you, trust that His love makes all of the 'ugly' go away. He can be trusted with your heart. His grace is so wonderful, that every sorrow that has contaminated your life, will be replaced, and the beauty that you thought was forever taken away, will be restored. The desire to quiet your pain forever must be changed! Silence ignores and justifies but speaking brings revelation so that every enemy will be known.

As a tool to heal, I release to you a much-needed voice that MUST be heard. So, Speak my Sisters! Speak your truth so that the world can hear!!

## *INTRODUCTION PART 2*
### *She Speaks Through Her Senses*

### *BREATHE*
Soul, release. Expel the pressure. Creature exhale.

Let go.

The impulse is excruciating. The fear controls and refuses to liberate.

The air is trapped.

The Creature floats in its human tank, slightly submerged, where the air remains captive.

To release the vapor and burst the surface may create a whirlpool of reactions, condemned.

To exhale could break the pain that the cavity holds, but the mind stresses to search for a renewed gasp.

If the Soul remains beneath this captivity of suffocation, death is inevitable.

Contemplate!!

Break the surface Creature or die encased in your own air.

She is the Creature, the Captive, the Soul.

She is afraid to release the trapped air because the reaction may create a 'ripple effect'. There are no receptacles sufficient to deal with the residual effects of her tidal wave.

She may be seen as a failure if she does not complete this path of self-denial that refuses to allow the freedom she needs to survive.

She repulses the temptation to satisfy her own needs by a guilty submission to cater to the desires of everyone around her.

And, She cannot. No, She will not. She refuses to live, because she may die.

Too afraid to try, too trapped to move, she cannot breathe, because she has no air.

Sympathetic resuscitation? Replaced by what? She does not know how to breathe without assistance, yet, she cannot wait for life support.

Besides, the creature is only a Woman, and why would she possibly need her own air? She wouldn't even know what to do with it!

Try her.

She knows.  She can.

She simply feels she needs permission.

### *SCREAM*

There is that age old question; "If a tree falls in the forest, does it make a sound?"  If there is no one to listen, is the crashing just as relevant?  Does the tree still desire the voice of its pain to be heard as well as the ground that receives its breaking?

If She screams, is the same true?  Does her voice ring vibrations in the ears of those around her, or is there a deafening from her significant sound?  Can She be heard?

She needs to be.

It is not insignificant chatter, it holds value.  She is a thinker, so She has weighed the validity before she considers its delivery.

Does Her tree fall to the ground with no one to listen? Does She have the ability to both recite and deduct all of the wisdom that is required in her significance?

What if no one hears?  What if there is no sound at

all? What if her sound is only muted by disregard?

Inquire, observe, and understand.

Speak your truth!

*You have a right to be heard!*
*Open your mouth and scream!!*
Even if no one is listening, YOU MUST hear your
own sound.

Your voice has been quieted for so long that it may
take the shock of its sound to shatter the noise barrier
and jumpstart your heart!!

**SO, SCREAM!**

**EVEN IF EVERYONE AND EVERYTHING**
**AROUND YOU SAYS YOU ARE INSANE.**
**YOU MUST SCREAM.**

**SCREAM UNTIL YOU CRY!! THEN SCREAM**
**AGAIN, UNTIL YOU LAUGH!!**
**VITAL RELEASE.**

**MEDICINAL.**

I scream, so that **YOU** can scream, so that **SHE** can
scream, so that **THEY** can scream, so that **WE** can
all be heard – eternally.

Now, be quiet, listen. And wait for the aftershock.

## *MARCH*

Feel! Respond!

Stop waiting for something to happen!!

You have blamed everyone else long enough!!

You have morphed into arthritic paralysis responding to your own stifling.

No one is holding you back!!

They can only halt your progress when you have given them the license to do so.

*MAKE IT HAPPEN.*
*MARCH!!*

Arise from your posterior mount and change your depressive bliss to something constructive.

Do not just respond out of responsibility.
**Enjoy the pleasure of movement**.
The walls were not purposed to become barriers of productivity. They were only temporary for the nesting of life created. The nest has been vacated.

Time to shift your productions to other arenas that demand your expertise.

You have settled for a sentence of emptiness that absorbs small pieces of you daily.

That is not 'marching to the beat of your own drum'. That, dear Creature is settling for being satisfied with a ghost of your former self. That is cheating the world from knowing your next layer.

***Not pretty enough, not smart enough, not stable, unprofessional, overweight, too broke?***

### *WORDS*

Empty words that you accept.

Words they say. Words you have the power to

extinguish.

What? You thought that you were finished. Not as

long as you are still breathing!

### *MOVE*

Shuffle those supporters you call feet and shift the air

into new dreams!!

Weight start dropping! Fear get out! Sore

bones, arthritic knees, depressed brows, hopeless

dreams, unfinished lives, broken hearts, empty days,

***BE GONE!***

Dear Creature, Precious Soul, take back your life. There is a beautiful life just waiting on the other side of the door.

## *LABELS*

You forgot to mention my name.  You only wanted to view me in a prison of my past or label me by my demise.  ***SAY MY NAME!!***

I no longer give you permission to disregard my

experience and make that pain my identity.

No! I demand that you acknowledge ME!

I am not just the women with the issue…, the one caught in adultery…, the raped…, the molested…, the evil…, the fat…, the tramp…, the mistake…, the #whateveryouthinkyouknowaboutmypast.

That is what happened, it is not who I am. Get to know me and get rid of the labels!

### *SAY MY NAME!!!*

# VOICE # 1

## *The Lost Journal of a Castaway*

Dear Diary,

*He hates me.*

The way he looks at me with those empty eyes, chills me to my bones. This silence between us is deafening. He says it is all my fault and while I understand why he doesn't want to talk; I need so desperately for him to speak.

*I am so lonely.*

**ALIENATED.**

*I cannot hear the soothing voice that spoke to us in the cool of the evening.*

Sitting outside in this vast emptiness, missing the delight of my garden home, *I am so lost*. Lost, from everything I knew. Lost, from the consoling touch of my husband, my friend. Lost, and empty. That light in his eye is gone. I remember how much he loved me. His hands always caressing me. His first words when the Master brought me to him expressed his delight at my beauty. I was his little 'Ishah', "bone of his bones, and flesh of his flesh". We were so close. Now, when he speaks to the Master, he refers to me as, "**that woman** you gave me."

## I feel UGLY.

Why did I listen? I am trying so desperately to recount that day. But it seems so cloudy now. I really didn't consider just one bite to be so terrible. I just felt like I had to taste it since the stranger said it would not kill me but only make me wise like the Master. I felt like it would not hurt anything to be just a little smarter.

THE MASTER'S INSTRUCTIONS WERE CLEAR!! I JUST DID NOT THINK!!

The stranger didn't seem that bad. He was so beautiful. I thought of him as a friend. I know now that his kind flattering words were only a ploy to cause me to forget my instructions, and then destroy me in the process. Once I took the first bite, it was so enticing that I could not stop myself. The feeling of something strange engulfed my body. It was as if, I knew it was wrong, but for the moment it felt good. Adam needs to taste this. Who told him that he would die? I am not dead.

## Or am I?

For a few moments, we thought the rush of heat that engulfed our insides was new, and different, but slowly, it felt like death. As we sat there confused and disoriented, the laughter of the stranger in the distance made both of us drop to the earth in fear!

Suddenly, I felt *exposed*. I looked at Adam and he looked at me with a totally different view that neither of us understood. The question in both of our eyes seemed to be, how can I face **Him**? I cannot let **Him** see me like this! I have never looked at myself this way. I must cover up. How did I not see this before?

***I'm sorry.***

*I can't stop crying.*

I feel like my head is going to explode! I just did not think it through.

***Why?***

That guardian will not let me back in my home. I can't get pass his sword!

It is so cold out here.

How do we start over?

Adam won't talk to me. When I approach him, he just says that he needs time to figure this out.

*I'm hungry.*

I miss the garden with all of its delicious fruits and pleasurable food. I didn't need that tree! I can recall the feeling of the grass under my feet that soothed and comforted me daily.  No worries, just contentment.

*I'm thirsty.*

This longing to quench a thirst inside is like something I have never experienced.  This dryness inside me is like a drought that the greatest rivers will not satisfy.

*It is so dark out here.*
*This darkness is heavy.*
**BLACK**
The peace of the night is replaced with sounds that I cannot recognize.

*I cannot breathe!*

Please daylight, come back. The animals have been behaving in such a strange way. A lion killed a lamb the other day.  I have never seen anything like this. I cannot escape the howls in the night.

*Daylight, please return.*
*I am so afraid.*

Subject to Adam?  Exactly what does that mean?
Pain in childbirth?  I don't really understand.
Oh!! Master, *I am sorry*!!  Can we please go back and start over?  I would scream and resist the temptation of that

stranger, that evil serpent. I thought he meant well, but he destroyed my life.

*I still feel that somehow the Master loves us, though I cannot hear His voice.*

**Please don't leave.**

**HELP!!**

Adam, please talk to me! Give me another chance.

He told me that I no longer have a voice in any matters. This is new. We always talked and did things with oneness. He no longer needs my voice.

**Is that subject?**

*I'm really hurting inside.*

What have I done? If Adam is so angry and he blames me, I realize that I will be held responsible by every generation to come. My children's children will ask why I reduced their heritage to labor, sorrow, and pain.

I'm sorry. I cannot say it enough. I scream it every hour, praying that the echo of my heart will reach a forgiving ear.

**I'M SORRY**!!

I must reach Adam. He must see me again. If I will be saved in bearing a child, I must get him to touch me again. But how?

**I AM DESPERATE**.

## I MUST FIGHT!!

So that future generations will have hope!


*Hear my cry, O God; attend unto my prayer. From the end of the earth will I cry unto thee, when my heart is overwhelmed: lead me to the rock that is higher than I. (Psalms 61:1-2 KJV)*

*Eve.*

# VOICE # 2

## *A Perpetual Cry for Justice*

*But every man is 'tempted', (a solicitation to evil) when he is drawn away of his own lust and enticed. Then when lust hath conceived, it bringeth forth sin: and sin, when it is finished, bringeth forth death. (James 1: 14-15 KJV)*

*The following story is based on true life events as told in the Old Testament of the Bible II Samuel chapter 13. The names have been omitted to protect the not so innocent.*

As we push open the doors of the courtroom, the fear churning in our stomachs ignites, as we meet the tumultuous atmosphere of the room. The madness of conflicting opinions fills the air coupled with the controversy of accusation. The invisible lines of division seem to violently split the room, resembling the accuracy of a boardroom arbitration.

Though the facts seem clear, it is obvious that by the cunning craftiness of these divisive, stoic men, this case will be presented in a manner that attempts to shift the jurors to support their corrupt thinking.

What did you have on!? How did you smell!? Why were you in that room!? How stupid could it have been to go into his room and not expect this virile young man to respond!? Why didn't you scream, young lady? Are you sure you did not want this to happen and then after your lusts were satisfied, is it not true that you knew the consequences, and what it looked like, so the only alternative was to cry rape!!?

## ANSWER ME!!

Your honor, council is badgering the witness, she is the victim here?!

*Sustained.*

Your honor, I am simply trying to get to the truth. This young man, full of so much potential, has his whole life hanging in the balance. So please, your honor, would you instruct *this girl* to **TELL THE TRUTH!!**

Eyes crimson and burnt from the days of humility and repulsive recount, she raises her head and opens her mouth to speak in her own defense, but the words refuse to cooperate. She takes a deep breath and finally divulges a noiseless grunt followed by more emptiness. She exhales deeply and says, *"I was..."*, but the tears are once again a tsunami of resentful grief. Her small physique slowly shrinks into obscurity as if she will disappear into herself, as her visual focus recoils to the floor beneath her. She is too terrified to glance across the room at her rapist, fearing that one optical meeting will cause her to relive each ugly moment of his vicious trespass.

Your honor, will you please instruct *this girl* to speak up!

Young lady, if you will not explain your side of the story, I am afraid that we will have no other choice than to assume that this young man is telling the truth.

Hearing the audacity of this demand, her grief shifts to appall, from appall to anger, and behind anger, a frightening strength swelled in her bosom. With all of the tenacity she could drag from her battered inner core, she sat up straight and somehow felt the strength of truth begin to build in her body. Out of the ashes, came a violent determination and understanding that this revelation would not only represent her future, she MUST speak, for every Daughter, Sister, Wife, or Mother in the future whose story would need to be spoken and heard, in order to survive.

She understood the longer that she sat in quiet isolation, this so called 'club', with all of its offensive members would continue to walk away holding the power and refusing to acknowledge their crimes as if they were only peccadilloes events. She knew that she must be the vehicle to promote a much-needed vindication that would catapult a turning point for all women, from every walk of life, and from every race, creed and color, for generations to come.

She wiped her tear stained face, steadied her vision with clarity, blew away the stale fluids that had taken residence in her nasal passage, and looked directly into the face of the man who she decided to snatch her power from. Then and there, she resolved that he would no longer be allowed to cradle the future of her existence in his unworthy hands. She bravely peered into the faces of all who beheld her, as if to say, "I will no longer give you permission to destroy my God-given-right to endure!"

*Your Honor, I sit here today adorned in sackcloth instead of the robes of a Princess. No longer allowed the vesture of honor but reduced to a barren desolate image of my former self. The pride of the virtuous has been stolen away, and I remain without hope of the fruitfulness of my femininity.*

*From a child I have desired to serve with great passion and accuracy. As a daughter of the king, his commands were my pleasure. With this said, it was not a hard task for me when my father requested that I assist my sick brother.*

*Upon entering my brother's home, I moved with swiftness and concern for his illness. With the love of a sister, I rushed to prepare a meal that I felt would help him to recover. I did not see the lustful stares that obviously were a camouflage of his real intent.*

**You knew what you were doing all of those years. Flaunting your virginity in my presence, making me want you as you pretended to ignore my stares!! Hearing my words of flattery and disregarding me day after day!!**

***Sit down sir, or I will hold you in contempt.***

*No Sir, your Honor. Why would I ever think that my brother, MY BROTHER, would look at me in such a lustful manner? When he demanded that everyone leave and asked me to feed him in his room, I only thought that the sickness must be getting worse. Besides, I was at my master's call and though I was a princess, a refusal by a woman of any sort was not allowed.*

*When he grabbed me and told me to lay with him, I knew he must be completely mad.* (the tears build in her ducts again, but out of sheer determination, she will not let them fall).

## Your Honor, is the court really buying this story!?

*I pleaded with him to not carry out such a horrific act, explaining that I would be hated, and he would be seen as a fool. But he never seemed to hear my words. Instead, he only became more violent as he rehearsed his unbridled love for me. My screams for mercy only seemed to drive him further into insanity. When my pleas would no longer work, he forced me to his bed and raped me.*

*Horrified at the unfolding of the last few moments, I raised myself from his bed and tried to make sense of everything. He screamed at me,* "**GET OUT!**" *He jumped up and covered himself as if I had dishonored him. I felt both hatred and contamination begin to move throughout my system. Not for him, your honor, but for myself.* **I hated me!! I felt dirty**!

*What? No, please do not shame me like this! Talk to the king, I pleaded. He will not deny you to marry me. But he did not listen. His anger only grew.* "*Guards! Throw this woman*

*out and lock the door". I cried uncontrollably. Please, my
brother, there is no cause for this! This evil in sending me
away is even worse than what you have already done. But
he ignored me, as his men slammed the door!
The echo of the bolt locking caused my bones to quake!!
Standing, locked outside of protection, and exposed to
complete embarrassment, I ripped what a few hours earlier
had been my garments of honor, into shreds. Without a hope
of a future, I wept sorely, for it was in essence, my death.*

*With my present plight of brokenness, I encountered those
of my household. Anger seemed to distort their faces as they
questioned my state.*

**Silence.**

*No concern for me. No wiping of tears.
No cleaning of the residue that would stain me for life.
No easing of the pain of my brutality ----------- just -------*

**Silence.**

*As if the calamity could be hushed away by this unspoken
censorship. The deafening sound of the silence pushed me
deeper into the insignificance that I bore. While instruction
demanded that it be quieted to protect him.*

**And ...**

*My brother moved forward without the simplest hesitation.*

*Your Honor, I sit here in shame while my oppressor is free. I suffer the condition of what is called unclean, while he celebrates his manhood like an unharnessed colt in flight. But as I sit here, a victim of this court, and a slave to the aura that rests over my head, I declare that my exploitation shall not be my end. I am settled by the grace of God and my own will power to release these chains from my throat that man designed to destroy me. For no matter the decision of this body of spectators here today, I declare, your Honor, that I am Free!*

*Tamar*

I empower every battered woman to face her truth with boldness! I support you in taking back every ounce of your womanhood snatched away by the predators of this world; and I decree and declare on this day, my Sisterhood, that you have the God given authority to release your past and embrace your future. Transform, my Sisters, in spite of the facts!! ----- you are free!!

The intent of presenting this court case is to allow the offended to finally have a much overdue voice. One of the best ways to equip young ladies to be aware of these unwarranted physical attacks, is to teach age appropriate language concerning their sexuality. Innocence is beautiful when it can be cultivated in the proper surroundings. But when exposed to the wickedness of the world, innocence is deadly.

No, this young woman probably should not have gone into the seclusion of the bedroom, *if* she understood the danger of lust. However, her comprehension of the order of life only saw a 'brother' and totally obliterated any trace of the danger of offence. This misinformed response to the danger landed her in a prison of isolation for the rest of her life. The innocent became the punished!

The only response to her violation comes two years later when the anger of one brother towards another results in death and the destruction of a family unit. He feels vindicated, but these events push her further into a social quarantine, that partner with guilt. Though she resolves to accept the blame as her own, it is once again the incorrect response of the men around her that disregard her feelings and respond in a manner that only satisfies a lust inside of them. This particular one being murder.

Case in point, please be aware, WE WANT YOU TO CARE, but many are silent because they do not TRUST your response.

So, we speak; to the men who do attempt to reach us with heart felt concern, please do so without a revengeful masculine brutality. That frightens us, usually because we desire to protect you. We need constructive protection that helps us heal. We need you to believe and not judge. We need for you to be just as appalled at this abuse as if you suffered the injustice.

# VOICE # 3

## *Unrequested Participation*

One of the most difficult positions that anyone can be put in, is to feel they have no say in things that directly affect their lives. Attempting to be a support system to someone, yet not being afforded any type of authority or opinion, except to follow, without question, is one that many women have struggled with for decades.

Living in the center of someone's dream or the destiny that they have on their life, and desiring to push them forward, often takes a complete walk of faith. The union established in the marital vows sets a stage for the dreamer to feel that life will always be an equally shared experience. However, the unfolding of this so called 'partnership' is often misleading and may be lacking in direction. The fact is decisions do not always manifest themselves in an equivalent manner. This leaves the partnership with the potential of becoming a 'dictatorship' instead.

Feeling as if you are being treated like a child and not afforded important information that governs the family, forces the spousal advocate to walk through their relationship in darkness. Many times, she is only included when there is a dilemma, and a report of failure is given. Then an expectation of an anchored shoulder is expected, without question or reservation. These actions may cause a supportive woman to feel that she only exists in his shadow, and that her assignment is to spend a lifetime building his aspirations with very little space to experience her own.

Women often graciously accept this role, but feel it is an injurious insult when they are not allowed any type of collaboration in what they support. The tragedy is, God created man and woman to be in a harmonious partnership. But this catastrophic separation usually leads to chaos and ends with the participants in their isolate corners contemplating divorce.

Sarah's desire to support her husband, the patriarch Abraham, and the blind journey he was on, was not always the easiest to accomplish. Can you imagine how hard it must have been to walk through a 25-year process (He was 75 and she was 65 when they first left Haran)? Abram was attempting to please God and to understand His direction. Though the promise was clearly given, its unfolding was not. However, without reservation, Sarai, followed quietly beside him all of the way. What Abram had, was his faith in a promise from God, and he believed that it would come to pass. This belief was acknowledged as righteousness. Sarai was not a part of the conversations that went on between Abram and God, yet, she had to follow suit through every aspect of the journey no matter what transpired in the process.

Many of the events would have no doubt been handled differently by her. She may have even had a different approach to the steps that Abram felt he was taking for their protection. Though Sarai supported Abrams love for Lot, she may have handled Lot differently if her mothering instincts would have been permitted.

It is important for us to understand that the characters in the Bible were not some sort of unique species. They were the same humans that we are. With this in mind, we must understand that just as we experience today, their desire to fulfill the call of God did not take some sort of magic trick, but it was a process. Just as we experience today, there are times when we all make mistakes and have to seek the face of God to get back on track.

Not everything that happens in the process of what we experience is handled properly even when we are striving to please God. We confront things by trial and error, praying that we are both hearing and responding correctly to what we feel God is saying to us. But many times, we are so far off base that we create situations that almost destroy us.

When Abram lied concerning Sarai being his sister the first time, (*Genesis 12:10-20*), the language of the Biblical text shows that he had his own preservation in mind.

> 1. *Behold now, I know that thou art a fair woman to look upon. Say, I pray thee thou art my sister: that it may be well with me for thy sake; and my soul shall live because of thee. (Genesis 12:11-12 KJV)*

Due to that curse, her beauty, Sarai was put in a position that could have compromised her honor and her piety. Upon seeing this beautiful woman, she is formally commended by the princess and taken to the house of Pharaoh. Abram is paid well and becomes quite rich. But the lie greatly displeased the Lord and he plagued Pharaoh's house, because of Sarai, Abram's wife. Abram escaped the anger of Pharaoh by God's intervention.

The second time, (*Genesis chapter 20*), Abraham gives a long explanation attempting to justify his decision to tell the same lie. Abraham fears for his own life. He explains that he and Sarah have the same father but not the same mother. This statement solidifies his claim. (During this era of the Bible, this type of marriage was permitted). However, it is not the marriage that he wishes to justify, but because of his fear of death, he reasons:

2.  *when God caused me to wander from my fathers'
    house, we agreed that this was the way that <u>she could</u>
    <u>show her love for me</u> (Genesis 20:13 KJV)*

Every place that they entered she was to say that Abraham was her brother so that **HE** would not be killed for **HER** beauty.

We must acknowledge that this behavior was selfish, and, in both cases, God was angry and warned those who had taken Sarah, to let her go. In both instances, the nations who had taken her to be a wife suffered great affliction and the threat of death. Egypt was plagued with great plagues, and the wombs of the women of Gerar were incapable of producing children as long as Sarah was in Pharaoh's house. In Gerar, the curse would not be lifted until Sarah was returned to Abraham and he offered to God a prayer of restoration.

Abraham receives a thousand pieces of silver and the king says to Sarah:

*"behold, he is to thee a covering of the eyes, unto all that are
with thee, and with all others: thus she was reproved."
(Genesis 20:16 KJV).*

The language of the text seems as if Sarah alone is being reprimanded. So, let us look at a different translation for a better understanding. The *New International Version* says the same portion of scripture like this:

*"I am giving your brother a thousand shekels of silver. This is to cover the offense <u>against you</u> before all who are with you; you are completely vindicated."* (cleared of blame or suspicion).

Needless to say, these were unwise decisions made by a righteous man. Decisions made without the welfare of Sarah being considered at all, and ones that she could not say 'no' to. Many suffered because of Abraham's fear and Sarah's beauty. Once again, beauty can be a curse and a platform for prejudice, instead of a blessing of honor.

I must acknowledge that though Sarah's virtue could have been compromised, God did not allow any type of defilement to come upon her. She was the anointed vessel preserved for His purpose and she *could not* be touched by foreign hands. Not foreign in the sense of nationality, (though this was true now that God had separated His people) but because she had to bear the royal seed that would develop a nation out of which Jesus would be born.

### *Unrequested Assistance*

According to Genesis, chapter 16, approximately ten years have passed for Abram and Sarai. Though they have been promised that their seed will be blessed beyond number, no children are present. Sarai feels the pressure mounting daily as the hope of her seventy-five-year-old body bearing a child seems to pass further away. Month after month, year after year, she hears the facts of the promise rehearsed in her ears. She, no doubt, wanders whether her role and value in this promise is valid. As time escapes, she feels the fruit of her fertility fade like a wicked clock ticking away the hours, each day with more vengeance than the day before. Desperation sets in and reason becomes tainted.

Intimacy is routine and tolerable at best as both she and her husband attempt to revitalize passion in their very seasoned bodies. What should be spontaneous love, becomes a tedious chore followed by the monotony of anticipated waiting.

Sarai is beginning to feel the acceptance of defeat in her barrenness. "The Lord has kept me from having children!! I cannot be the hindrance that holds Abram back." Hopelessness leads to despair as a feeling of urgency makes her desperate to do something to assist Abram and God in accomplishing this promise.

The social status of a woman bearing children assured her prestige in the Jewish community. This fact was true whether the birth was characterized by a promise or not. To be a barren woman labeled her as invaluable.

Many times, women accept their lot in life, hiding the pain and pursuing a mindset that allows them to move forward with another plan. They will do anything to show support. Behind it, however, they go unnoticed because they do so in a manner that camouflages the sorrow inside and makes everyone believe that they are content. This fact has been true throughout history.

Analyze the women within your peer group. How often do you really know what they face on a daily basis? We train and have been trained to accept life as it comes with all of the grace we can muster. If it presents us with obstacles, we learn to take the obstacles and build walls. The problem is, we cannot allow the walls that we build to protect and preserve us to become our own tombs. Women are taught to always have a solution. You are not considered innovative unless you can juggle all of life's issues and still face the world looking like a super model. These demands are unfair, unrealistic, and inhumane.

Fortunately, when it comes to what God has presented as His assignment on your life, He needs no assistance in fulfilling

His plan. *"For I know the plans I have for you, says the Lord..." (Jeremiah 29:11 NLT)*. He loves taking what seems impossible and transforming it into a miracle.

We are not afforded the privilege of knowing how long Sarai contemplated the idea of a surrogate. Was she the innovator of a new idea that would affect the world? Watching and absorbing her husband's frustration made her desperate to come up with a solution that she felt would work. She did not discuss the ins and outs of her plan. She waited and weighed her options and without hesitation blurted out her agenda to Abram.

*Now Sarai, Abram's wife, had borne him no children. But she had an Egyptian slave named Hagar; so she said to Abram, "The Lord has kept me from having children. Go, sleep with my slave; perhaps I can build a family through her." Abram agreed to what Sarai said... Sarai took her slave and gave her to her husband to be his wife. He slept with Hagar, and she conceived. When she knew she was pregnant, she (Hagar) began to despise her mistress (Sarai). (Genesis 16:1-4 NIV)*

What seemed like a solution when she was pressed to move forward has now turned into an idea gone completely wrong! Whenever we attempt to provide an answer, when the only person with the answer is God, we will always end up digging a deeper tunnel of despair.

*For wherever there is jealousy and selfish ambition, there you will find disorder and evil of every kind. (James 3:16 NLT)*

Whenever you make a huge decision, always take time to think it through from every angle. It is obvious that Sarah laid out her plans with a sort of tunnel vision. When we do that, we fail to see the big picture. We only see what is in front of us. Come on ladies, we all know that opening up your bedroom to another woman is declaring war!

### *A Bad Situation Turned Worse*

There is a special bond that happens when a man and woman really want to experience childbirth. For Hagar, it was the blessing of a child that now, only has the shadow of Sarai to contend with. For Abram the birth was, no doubt in his mind, the final manifestation of the unfolding of God's promise. *For Sarai!!!* Imagine what this seventy-five-year-old woman must have felt like. Waiting outside of the tent for what seemed like hours, while she hears the moans of passion and delight, that she cannot control. Her husband now spending all of his intimate time with this much younger, vibrant, fruitful, woman. The screams of pregnant delight as she gives Abram the desire of his heart. This woman, *Hagar*, that is now expressing her hatred of the person who not only gave her this newfound joy but is now in the way of she and her 'baby daddy' enjoying their life.

Can you embrace what she is feeling?  Being left out!!  No place for her in the equation at all!  AND - Just because Sarai was outside of the tent did not mean that she no longer felt sexual herself.  What a mess!!

And the sad part is, Sarai put Hagar in her husbands' arms herself, and Abram did not turn her down.  All of the years that Sarai did not have a voice, but when she gave the suggestion of him being with Hagar, there was no resistance whatsoever.  Now, Sarai has to appear to be the evil one and demand that Hagar be cast out.  She blames Abram for the situation, and notice, he does not <u>even</u> have the nerve to argue with her.

*Then Sarai said to Abram, you are responsible for the wrong I am suffering.  I put my slave in your arms, and now that she knows she is pregnant, she despises me.  May the Lord judge between you and me.*

**Abraham responds**:

*Your slave is in your hands, Do whatever you think best
Then Sarah mistreated Hagar; so she fled from her.*

*Verse 9: Then the angel of the Lord told her, "Go back to your mistress and submit to her." (Genesis 16)*

My Sisters, God is not in those bad decisions that we make, even when we think we are helping the situation.  That assistance was *UNREQUESTED!*  Hagar returned and submitted to her mistress as God instructed her, but we all know that the tension between them never went away.

Hagar has her son Ishmael when Abram is eighty-six years old. So, Sarai is seventy-six. Still beautiful, still barren, but an empty shell of a woman, hanging on the memory of a promise.

Let me take this moment to speak to my Sisters who know what it feels like to possess all of the potential in the world and to feel you have absolutely nothing to show for it. Even to the wives that have husbands in a powerful position, and you are left to feel like an artifact in the corner with the purpose of making someone else shine. God has not forgotten what He placed upon your life in the course of this assignment. Even if you feel ignored, unimportant, or useless. Ladies, *THAT'S A MAN THING, NOT A GOD THING!!* That statement is not to bash men. What I mean is that humans have a survival instinct to look out for themselves when striving to achieve. Stop being left in that corner, girl! Find out where *YOUR* place is and go to work. But do so by first seeking the order of God and you will not fail!! Sarai's problem was that she left the order of God and did things her own way.

No wonder, when the angel appeared 14 years later, changing Abram's name to Abraham (father of many nations), and Sarai (princess) to Sarah (mother of many nations), and informing him that Sarah would have a baby in nine months, Abraham laughed, and so did Sarah. The angel's rebuke of the laughter made Sarah lie and then she denied doing so.

Do not criticize her!! We all get weary in waiting. If a prophesy is given to us and it does not manifest within what we see as a reasonable time, we start to doubt and label those who spoke to us as a lying prophet. So, Sarah laughing over a prophesy given twenty-five years prior, is not hard to understand. She was laughing at what she felt was she and Abraham's inability. Listen to the language of their debate:

**To Abraham:**
*...Sarah shall her name be. And I will give thee a son also of her; yea, I will bless her, and she shall be a mother of nations; kings of people shall be of her. Then Abraham fell on his face, and laughed, and said in his heart, Shall a child be born unto him that is an hundred-years- old? And shall Sarah, that is ninety-years-old bear?*

*O that Ishmael might live before thee!*

*And God said, Sarah thy WIFE shall bear thee a son indeed; and thou shall call his name Isaac: and I will establish my COVENANT with him for an everlasting covenant, with his seed after him.*

*And as for Ishmael, I have heard thee...But my covenant I will establish with Isaac... (Genesis 17:15-21 KJV)*

**To Sarah**:
*Now Abraham and Sarah were old and well stricken in age; and it ceased to be with Sarah after the manner of women. Therefore Sarah laughed within herself, saying, After I am waxed old shall I have pleasure, my lord also being old? And the Lord said unto Abraham, Wherefore did Sarah laugh, saying Shall I of a surety bear a child, which am old? Is there anything too hard for the Lord?*

*At the time appointed, I will return unto thee, according to the time of life, and Sarah shall have a son. Then Sarah denied, saying I laughed not; for she was afraid. And he said, Nay, but thou didst laugh. (Genesis 18:11-15 KJV)*

Laughter. What we often do when we do not understand. What we sometimes do to keep from shedding tears. Laughter. What we use to disguise our real truth. What we use to survive, that which is impossible to comprehend. Laughter!!

Sarah was ninety years old, she no longer had a menstrual cycle, and the dryness of age no longer allowed her pleasure with Abraham. We do not really know at this point if intimacy even mattered. She had probably built different interest in the thirteen years since Ishmaels birth. She, no doubt, had settled into the separate life Abraham lived with Hagar and Ishmael, as he attempted to be a good father and mentor his son. Remember, Abraham has also settled upon Ishmael being his promise and the seed of his manhood. It is not until the angel appears with this new information that the suggestion of the original promise is reiterated.

The response to this new prophesy left such a mark, that the name given to Abraham for his seed of promise is, Isaac, meaning "laughter".

*And Abraham was an hundred years old, when his son Isaac was born unto him. And Sarah said, "God hath made me to laugh, so that all that hear will laugh with me". And she said, "Who would have said unto Abraham, that Sarah should have given children suck? For I have born him a son in his old age. (Genesis 21:5-7 KJV)*

### *Get Out!*

It did not take long for the atmosphere to shift. Holding her own baby in her arms, Sarah now has ammunition to take back her territory. She now can reclaim what she lost almost fifteen years earlier. Believe me, she did so with a territorial vengeance. She quickly informs Abraham that this 'son of a slave', *shall not* be heir with my son! Cast this bondwoman and her son out!! Of course, Abraham was very sorrowful concerning this. Ishmael was his son that he also loved. However, to keep this spirit of strife among them would have probably detoured Abraham from his walk of faith.

*It is better to live in a small corner on the roof than to share the house with a woman who is always arguing." (Proverbs 21:9 ERV)*

Sarah is content that God has given her what seemed impossible. He speaks to Abraham confirming Sarah's request:

*And God said unto Abraham, "Let it not be grievous in thy sight because of the lad, and because of thy bondwoman; in all that Sarah hath said unto thee, hearken unto her voice, for in Isaac shall thy seed be called. And also of the son of the bondwoman shall I make a nation, because of thy seed. (Genesis 21:12 KJV)*

Understand, Hagar was considered a second wife, and her son was the only one that Abraham had to bond with for over fourteen years. This had to be a very hard task to have to face. Sarah did not care!! She would not allow Isaac's heritage to be affected or shared with this bondwoman and her son. Ishmael mocked Isaac; they were cast out!!

Once again, this is what happens when we try to plan, without direction. Yes, it would have been a long exhausting wait for Sarai and Abram. But so many things could have been avoided, if they would have waited. Down through history, and even today the fight between these brothers' heritage still exists.

The moral of the story, my Sisters, learn to wait!! Weigh your options before your reactions create situations for your future, that are much worse than the present or the past. Learn to trust the God that creates the plan. You do not always have to be in control or understand the outcome. Learning to wait, is learning to trust. Putting each of these into practice is the journey towards a stress-free life. Wait for God to allow the time for your voice to be acknowledged.

# VOICE # 4

## *I Can't Wait to be Grown!!*

My name is Dinah. It means "Vindicated or Judged"

I am so tired of everyone telling me what to do! It is bad enough that I am seldom allowed beyond our tents but having twelve brothers who think they can boss me around is even worse. Don't get me wrong, I know they want to protect me, but I am old enough to take care of myself. They just don't want me to have any fun.

I want to be like the other girls that I see. They look so beautiful with all of their fancy clothes and jewelry. I hear the laughter and screams sometimes at night when they have their festivals. They are having so much fun! And I can just imagine all of the boys!

It is too quiet around here. It seems that all my family is concerned about are my brothers and their constant drama. My mom and my aunt are always bickering. Dad just seems absent from opinion. No one even notices me. You seldom even hear my name.

I work and run behind them, submitting myself to the rules they have set for me, but, oh how I long to get away and breathe. I bet that if I waited until they were all busy, I could slip away for a little while and get back before anyone even noticed. I wish I had the nerve! I am so bored!!

That is how I felt as a young girl. I was so enticed by what I did not know. I saw the seclusion and safety provided by my family as punishment. When I was told to stay out of Shechem, and away from traditions that I did not understand, I thought that my family was only trying to deny me some sort of privileges, in an effort to keep their only girl hidden away like a little treasure. I now understand that when parents say they want to protect you, they see something ahead that you do not have the maturity to comprehend. This maturity is not always about age, it is more often about experience.

I share my story, so that girls in the future will understand that having a covering over their life is a blessing. Don't always be so eager to throw it away. The world is so cruel, especially for girls, and it has been that way from my day to yours. So please, take heed, listen, and learn from my experience. I did manage to slip out.

The air of freedom felt so wonderful as the heat of the sun warmed my body. As I reached the Shechem borders, even the aroma of the atmosphere seemed to shift as it seduced me further into this culture. I must have stuck out to them as much as they did to me since our cultures were so diverse. They seemed to notice me immediately as they drew closer.

I wanted to see and experience everything that I felt secluded from. There, finally breathing the air I had longed for, I felt welcomed by those who desired to couple their curiosity with mine. Other girls, like myself, who wandered around carefree. Wide-eyed and adventurous, attempting to embrace and partake of everything they encountered. It was like a dream.

I did not feel the gulf that was forming between me and home. I was just so happy to be free and doing whatever I desired, without limits. Soon, I forgot about home and fell victim to the calamity of a culture that I did not know. It did not take long for the dream to become a NIGHTMARE! I had never had any man look at me the way that he was. ME!

The Prince of the city was looking at me. He is so cute. But I'm afraid. Though I feel flattered by his attention, it makes me feel somewhat uncomfortable. Almost dirty. I feel butterflies in my stomach. I have watched my brothers all of my life and been somewhat repulsed by their behavior. But look at him. He moves so differently. He is so mature. Wait. Is he coming over here? What am I supposed to do? Oh my! My name? My name is Dinah. I came from the Hebrew camp.

What do you mean, bring me to you? Excuse me, take your hands off of me! "I didn't hurt you, did I?" I could not bring myself to speak. I had allowed myself to be put in a situation where I was stuck. This prince had the power to take me like prey and I could not do anything about it! What will my family say? Surely, by now they realize I'm gone.

He is not cruel. He says that he loves me. But color it however you want, it was rape, not love. I did not ask for this! He says he will make it right and ask my father to marry me. Now you ask? This is not the way that we do things at home. I guess I will have to learn to be content. My life must now be sold to his.

The buzz of conversation throughout the palace indicates to me that Prince Shechem has presented his plans of marriage to his father, Hamor. He becomes the mediator to my father Jacob, for the intent of his son. The insult behind what Shechem and Hamor are trying to camouflage as honor infuriates my brothers. Coupled with their rage is a sense of grief.

Love? No, you have wrought folly in Israel against a daughter of Jacob, against our sister, and this type of behavior will not be accepted.

Hamor pleads with my father and brothers; "The soul of my son Shechem longs for your daughter. Please give her to him to be his wife." Let there be peace. We will give you our daughters to marry and we will marry yours, and all live together in harmony. Please, we will do whatever you request to make this possible.

I thought that it was all settled when my brothers, Simeon and Levi, struck a deal with the men of the city. A deal? Nothing was said to me about it. How am I supposed to feel? I don't know if I love him, but he has taken away my gift and left me without a choice, and here I sit again, ignored by my brothers!

They murdered them all!! I feel guilty. None of this should have happened!! No one will want me now. My brothers feel vindicated. He had no right to treat our sister like a harlot!! My father is angry. He fears a rebellion is possible. Me? I feel used.

Their Prince is dead, and with him went my status as a Princess. I should have stayed in the safety of home and waited for my 'prince' to find me. My name is Dinah, and you will never hear my name again.

Often, the world lies in wait for the innocent to bring them to destruction. Be content in your journey and take each step with caution. No, you cannot spend your entire life in the security of home, but you must be secure in your plans. A bad choice can leave its residue for a lifetime. Many girls left their security prematurely only to have to return in shame. Cherish the coverings that have been invested over you. Many do not have them. I pray that someone invests in you as well. However, when you do have that security, hold on to it forever. Even a grown-up little girl needs to know that she is protected!

*(Please read the vital information listed at the end of the book concerning runaways\*\*)*

# VOICE # 5

## *The Beauty and The Beast*

*Do not be yoked together with unbelievers. For what do righteousness and wickedness have in common? Or what fellowship can light have with darkness? What harmony is there between Christ and Belial? (Satan) Or what does a believer have in common with an unbeliever?*
*(2 Corinthians 6:14-15 NIV)*

Wealth coupled with wickedness causes a person to be unreasonable. When you are allotted the privileges that great wealth brings, you are seldom held accountable. If fate pushes you towards punishment, the wealthy say, "I can buy my way out of this". There are always followers who condone any amount of bad behavior just to be carted along on the journey of unbridled wealth. Unfortunately, as seen in the example of the 'prodigal son', when wealth is gone so are the supporters. It is with this thought that many extremely wealthy individuals, especially men, guard their riches in an effort to keep a certain amount of control. Nabal, wasted his riches on his own riotous pleasure, but was stingy when it was time to show charity.

We have all encountered individuals who are financially sound but would not bless another person if their lives depended on it. They are willing to benefit from the labor of others, but the acknowledgement of a job well done is simply beneath them. They respond to those who have favored and blessed them as if they are owed certain privileges simply because of who they are. Not realizing that no matter how high your position, at a moment's notice, life can abruptly change. Your life may seem to be untouchable by man, but by the swift judgement of the Almighty God your life can be altered forever. And every one of those who you disdained and abused will be left to enjoy the pleasure of what you left behind.

No little girl grows up hoping that her destiny lands her in the arms of a brutish, evil, foolish, and unloving man. Years of preparation in education and poise, and training to carry herself in an appealing and virtuous manner, drives her to hopefully be seen as valuable and precious. She does not aspire to live out her existence cleaning up the messes that he so unthoughtfully creates, always having to compensate with a smile, in hope of camouflaging the brutal language that spills from his mouth without reservation. She does not desire to be shunned by society because of his lack of ability to approach even the slightest issues with tact. However, his arrogant approach toward his fellow man unfortunately groups her in the consideration of also being shunned, resulting in a life of misery.

No little girl wakes up yearning for this to be her fate, yet many suffer, often in silence at the mercy of those who would judge her character by his brute.

**Fate**: *The course of someone's life; or the outcome of a particular situation for some, seen as beyond their control. Lot, destiny, portion, doom; An inevitable and often adverse outcome, condition, or end.*

How did I get here? Each day, this man lives out the character of his name. FOOL! *(Nabal)*. Despite the fact that his lifestyle attempts to steal every ounce of the respect that I have tried to keep at the forefront of this tumultuous relationship, I must try to love him. My family felt this arrangement with his wealth would be to my benefit. So, with little power to resist, I exist in this bitter reality. There have been many days that I wanted to run, but since it was chosen for my destiny to be locked in his, I stay.

I stay, praying that one day he will change. But each day of his bitter treatment makes it seem as though life's kindness has turned a deaf ear. I CANNOT LEAVE!! My godly commitment and vow refuses to release me. However, no matter the commitment, the turmoil refuses to go away. OH, MY GOODNESS, HE STINKS!! Vomiting the mixture of drunkenness and the leftover residue of forbidden love from his weekend gala. His demanded advances towards me are met with resistance in his present state. I refuse to follow his adulterous depravity. Oh no, please do not touch me!! Move over!! I cannot abide this rancid odor.

I have begged him to resist the temptation of these satanic ventures. But each week brings a different group of well-wishers to justify his evil behavior. His lusts outweigh his love and respect for our vows.

This union was not negotiated with a spiritual mind. Could those who chose for me not see beyond his ability to give me anything they felt I needed? Anything, that is, except love and respect. His lust for wealth and prestige has developed a controlling monster who never even considers godly principles and direction. While I lay in humble submission to the order that governs my godly upbringing, each encounter with my husband becomes more challenging. His dismissive responses only further alienate our already volatile relationship. He thinks that because he is rich, I should be content, but it's not enough.

So, I stay here. Enduring this shame, afraid of the bitterness that increasingly swells in my belly each day. A cringe of irritation crawls up my spine and causes me to tremble when

I hear him bellow out 'ABIGAIL"!! I pray that he is too drunk to perform so that I may be spared his repulsive embrace that only leaves him comatose, and me, empty. In fear of Gods' displeasure, I ask myself, do I hate this miserable existence, or do I hate him?

## *Abigail*

He did what?! I have heard that this great captain and his men guarded and protected the flocks for many days. Does this husband of mine understand the insult of his behavior in not respecting this simple request for victuals? He is laying in the parlor basking in his week of unbridled lust, unaware that our fate lies in the hands of angry, famished, soldiers who have a right to be disgruntled. I will make haste and prepare for them, praying that they will receive this kindness and not bring destruction on us.

Oh my God, if I live through this, please help him to change. Please do not allow my fate to be swallowed up in the sin of my husband. Don't allow the anger of these men to bring harm to your servant. I know that I should have never connected with this man whose pleasures are for a worldly taste and not for you. But I really thought I could get him to change.

Forgive me. Show me how to live in this evil existence and please protect me from the life that he has chosen to include me in. Lord, I cannot change him, only you can. If he does not want change, then please, deliver me from this prison of fear.

### Nabal

*Who is this fellow David?" he sneered. Who does this son of Jesse think he is? There are lots of servants these days who run away from their masters. Should I take my bread and my water and my meat that I've slaughtered for my shearers and give it to a gang who comes from God knows where? (I Samuel 25:10-11 TLB)*

### David

*"Get your swords", was David's reply as he strapped on his own. (I Samuel 25:13a TLB)*

### Servant to Abigail

*But David's men were very good to us and we never suffered any harm from them; in fact, day and night they were like a wall of protection to us and the sheep, and nothing was stolen from us the whole time they were with us. You'd better think fast, for there is going to be trouble for our master and his whole family. He is such a stubborn lout (an uncouth and aggressive man) that no one can even talk to him! (I Samuel 25:16-17 TLB)*

### David

*A lot of good it did to help this fellow. We protected his flocks in the wilderness so that not one thing was lost or stolen, but he has repaid me bad for good. All I get for my trouble is insults. May God curse me if even one of his men remains alive tomorrow morning. (I Samuel 25:21-22 TLB)*

We enter into an exchange of vows hoping to live out a fairytale dream of marital bliss. Often, we know that things are not perfect from the beginning. However, that motherly instinct of nurturing clicks in, and even if the circumstances are minimal at best, we believe that we can fix it. The problem, my Sisters, is that you cannot keep placing a bandage on what refuses to be healed. Unfortunately, we cannot and will not accept this fact until we have been abused, torn, ridiculed, and dragged through the ringer of humiliation. Then, once all hope seems to be lost, we regretfully search for a way out of something that sound council could have helped us avoid.

*...in the multitude of counsellors there is safety (Proverbs 11:14 KJV).* With the exception of a few countries, we no longer live in a society of arranged marriages. The day of 'shotgun weddings' has ceased. If it happens, you allowed it to. Otherwise, forced marriage is considered bondage and slavery.

Desperation and loneliness are not good reasons to feel that marriage is the answer. Marriage is not a fairytale, it is WORK! We must stop allowing our young ladies to think that Prince Charming is going to ride up on a white horse and whisk them away into the sunset. That only happens in a Disney or Dream Works movie. Even in this text about Abigail, David was not riding up to sweep her away. He was on his way to kill her and her wicked husband and everything connected with them. When she eventually ends up with David, she was really considered part of the spoils as a result of Nabal's death. God turned the circumstances around for her good, but the beginning was not so.

I am not saying that your dream of a wonderful marriage is not possible. I am saying that in order for that to happen, you will have to put the work in. And no, money is not the solution to every problem. As a matter of fact, there are more rich people divorcing and unhappy than there are people who had to work hard through the years and struggle *together* to *build* a life. Those are the marriages that usually stand the test of time and fifty years later the couples are still together celebrating in the society page of the newspaper. Now before you get frustrated, there are always exceptions, but the majority will find many of these statements to be true.

I come from a generation where men believed they were the support and covering of their wives. This generation of men boldly tell me, 'she must bring something to the table.' I know that reading that may make you ask, what is wrong with that? I agree that the days of simply being 'barefoot and pregnant' are long gone. I am happy about that fact!! But that is not what I mean. They tell me, if she does not have a certain amount of money, if she doesn't have a certain job status, if she isn't a certain size, etc. she is unacceptable. You may still ask, what is wrong with that? Well, then in fairness, I must ask, what are his stats? A man cannot look at his bride as if she were simply trying to, 'take his stuff'!! How long have women taken a man with a bicycle and not a penny to his name and waited for the better day, while people laughed at him, but she saw his potential? These are worldly concepts that do not follow the order of God. Times have changed, you say, that is so true, but at the end of the day we must decide who we will submit to. God or man? God always intended for marriage to be a partnership and not a war zone to establish sides.

These same men will easily concur that a woman *must* 'obey' them. When Adam and Eve were in the Garden of Eden, before the fall, they were equal partners. After the expulsion from the garden, everything shifted, and Eve had to become subject to Adam. She had to submit to his authority as the man and accept him as her direction, following him as he rules. This was her curse.

*...thy desire shall be to thy husband, and he shall rule over thee. (Genesis 3:16 KJV)*

When Jesus died for the sin of Adam, He broke the curse of sin and bondage over our heads. He opened a new possibility of life that mirrored His first love of humanity. When we are baptized in the name of Jesus and receive the gift of the Holy Spirit, we participate in that death, burial, and resurrection that creates a new life separated from the stain of Adamic sin. The middle wall of partition that separated man from entering the holy place of God was torn down from top to bottom allowing us to enter into His grace. Every curse held against man is washed away by the blood of Jesus. If every other curse is lifted, then why would God leave that one curse to bind women? The regenerated woman of God now practices the grace of submission taught in the New Testament by an act of LOVE and HONOR and not a CURSE.

*(Dispensation Class 2019 taught by Bishop H. A. Seaton. For additional information, please read Matthew 27:51; Hebrews 4:16; and Ephesians chapter 2).*

Now for those who do not believe or understand this, the question becomes what about 'pain in childbirth' and 'working by the sweat of his brow'? Those are the *processes* now developed in a *world* that has been cursed. The blood bought child of God lives in a world of evil and destruction, but this is no longer your identity or destiny. The regeneration of the Baptism and the Holy Spirit prepares you for a transformation to a higher level that does not exist in this realm. It is obtained here on Earth by an act of faith in the Word of God that leads to salvation and is lived out in the presence of His glory, with exceeding joy in the heavenlies!! That participation brings revelation to the following scriptures. (Please take the time to read this entire chapter that will bring great enlightenment).

*[14]I have given them thy word; and the world hath hated them, because they are not of the world, even as I am not of the world. [15] I pray not that thou shouldest take them out of the world, but that thou shouldest keep them from the evil. [16]They are not of the world, even as I am not of the world. [17]Sanctify them though thy truth: thy word is truth. [20]Neither pray I for these alone, but for them also which shall believe on me through their word. (St. John 17:14-17, 20 KJV)*

Kosmos: (Greek) world system; order. In the New Testament - organized humanity. The world of "men"
Thalassa: (Greek) Unorganized Humanity; the mere "mass of men" (*The Scofield Commentary Bible*)

*... ye are from beneath; I am from above: ye are of this world; I am not of this world. (John 8:23 KJV)*

Thank God for the covering of godly women. The ones that learn to pray and to intercede. The ones who know how to smooth over the worse situations and bring peace. She has an ability to speak in softness and turn those things that could be disasters into peace. She is willing to put herself in jeopardy to spare her family from any harm. This woman knew how to assemble together the 'stuff' that could satisfy her oppressor, yet, never be missed by an abusive, stingy husband who may have punished her for her charity. But this godly woman understood both the protocol and the respect in these matters. Though her husband's behavior appalled her, her respect for him pushed her to cover him.

### Abigail to David

In godly respect she approached this future king stating;

*[24]I accept all the blame in this matter, my lord. Please listen to what I have to say. [25]Nabal is a bad-tempered boor, (unrefined and ill mannered) but please don't pay any attention to what he said. He is a fool just like his name means. But I didn't see the messengers you sent. [26]Sir, since the Lord has kept you from murdering and taking vengeance into your own hands, I pray by the life of God and by your own life too, that all your enemies shall be cursed as Nabal is. [27]And now, here is a present I have brought to you and your young men. [28]Forgive me for my boldness in coming out here. The Lord will surely reward you with eternal royalty for your descendants, for you are fighting His battles; and you will never do wrong throughout your entire life. [29]Even when you are chased by those who seek your life, you are safe in the care of the Lord your God…But the lives of your enemies shall disappear like stones from a sling. [30]When the Lord has done all of the good things, He promised you, and has made you king of Israel, [31]you won't want the conscience of a murderer who took the law into his own hands! And when the Lord has done these great things for you, please remember me, your servant!" (I Samuel 25:24-31 TLB)*

### *David's response to Abigail*

*[32]Bless the God of Israel who has sent you to meet me today! [33]Thank God for your good sense! Bless you for keeping me from murdering the man and carrying out vengeance with my own hands. [34]For I swear by the Lord, the God of Israel who has kept me from hurting you, that if you had not come out to meet me, not one of Nabal's men would be alive tomorrow morning. [35]Then David accepted her gifts and told her to return home without fear, for he would not kill her husband. (I Samuel 25:32-35 TLB)*

God moved on Nabal's behalf without him even realizing the risk his wife had taken for him to be alive. However, God is not going to always allow the innocent to suffer behind the foolishness of the wicked.

When Abigail returned home, she may have hoped that this divine intervention that quieted the anger of David may have somehow bled over into the culture of her home. But back to the halls of reality, she walks in only to find that her husband has thrown yet another big party. There he lies, rip roaring drunk. What disappointment must have dropped in her belly. What disgust over an atmosphere that seemed as if it would never change.

By the morning, he lies in a sober state, no doubt suffering the illness of his leftover folly. Abigail began to rehearse to her husband all of the trauma of the previous day and what she had done to stop the calamity they were doomed for. As she solemnly recounted every event, Nabal was so overtaken in fear that he suffered a stroke and lay paralyzed for ten days. With no recovery in sight, he died. But the Bible says that the Lord killed him!! Proof that as spoken in a prior chapter, god has a specific time when he will stop the hand of your enemy. Trust him!!

God will only allow us to be tried for a season. He gives the offender a space for repentance. Abigail did not pray for the death of her wicked husband, she walked through her dilemma with grace. But she understood that Nabal could not continue his evil behavior without eventually ending up either killing himself or falling under the judgement of God. When David heard that Nabal was dead, he responds in worship, Praise the Lord! God has kept me from doing it myself; he has received his punishment for his sin. David wasted no time, but immediately sent for Abigail and made her his wife. She readily agreed to his request.

Abigail now marries by her own choice to say, "yes". It is not a perfect union. She marries David in faith, not questioning. Though David did not even have a house of his own, she knew that the promise of God to him, would over time, be fulfilled. Her wealth from her previous marriage became a blessing to help David in meeting his obligations. They WORKED TOGETHER to fulfill Gods' plan for their lives. Abigail is beside David as he seeks refuge in Philistine territory, she is captured and rescued in Ziklag, and later settles with David in Hebron, where she has his son, Chileab.

We see the destruction that comes along with being unequally yoked. Prayers need to be released on the behalf of all of the women who spend a lifetime locked in the bondage of an unbeliever or a believer who will not be led by the Holy Spirit. Many women have held their heads up with great poise as they suffered without relief. It is imperative that we slow down the process that sends us into the wrong arms.

It is just as devastating to spend your youth in terror and then end up later living a life alone. A life full of sadness, loneliness, and unfulfillment. When you have given every ounce of your being and still are left in the wake of devastating dishonor. Abandoned because of someone that they felt was better, someone, that fulfilled a greater lust, leaving you feeling empty and struggling with low self-esteem.

Devastated. And now, your entire existence is endless days of trying to dig out of the ruins. God has something so much better just a little further down the road. Every side bar further lengthens the wait. Just stand still for a moment, make yourself the best you can be, and wait to see what God is in the process of sending to you. He desires for His daughters to be whole, and He knows that many of them have been horribly treated. However, He never wants the errors of a bad relationship to put us further in devastation by our own bad response. Living a self-desecrating life of exploitation in retaliation to your pain only hurts you and leaves the world to judge. It seemingly justifies the ill treatment that was given to you by an unapologetic spouse. Do not allow that to happen in the midst of your pain! It is only adding insult to injury.

Love yourself beyond your pain and let God handle the vengeance. Trust me it will work out better that way. It may seem that the offender is getting by, but God never forgets. And just be ready, because you never know, if God decides that you are to minister them to wholeness, they may have to come right back to you to be whole. Just know, God will not ask you to endure, what He will not equip you to handle.

# VOICE #6

## *Refusal: Defiance or Integrity?*

Denying acceptance and welcoming the truth of your own voice gives a liberation to the mind, body, and soul; but it may come with great cost.

I am furious! This must be a dream, no, a nightmare! He cannot be serious!! What is it that he expects me to do? Flaunt and bear myself before him and his drunken friends?

Where is the respect and the dignity that should be afforded to me as the queen? I know that I will receive the damnation of the royal league if I refuse, but I will be robbed of my vesture of pride if I comply. What have I been left with? Surrounded by every other wife who waits attentively for my response to this demand, I feel the weight of responsibility that has just been tattooed on my head. Does the future of this sisterhood of victimized creatures wait for my response that restlessly awaits my permission to escape? I hear their air trapped in captivity as they wait to breathe either sighs of relief or gasps of fear.

I must articulate my disgust at this request by repudiating even the slightest inkling of flattery. I do not accept the insistence that he is proud of the beauty and fairness of his queen that only compliments his wealth. No, this is the rude perversion of a drunken mob that would have me bear my beauty like a harlot. The order is to bear the crown alone. Will their eyes behold its wealth, or my unveiled body? I cannot bear this thought.

Where is the protection that should shield me from those who would deliberately put me on display in such a perverse and unreasonable, manner despite the consequences? This simply cannot be the same man who held me in his arms and made me feel as if I were the most precious women he had ever encountered. This is his need to appear relevant coupled with his fear to deny men of selective indifference. They have no conscience of good or evil. They only desire to indulge in flexing their insignificant power by whatever fancies the moment.

The echo of this maddening crowd of repulsive men, anticipating my arrival is deafening. It spills down every corridor of these palace halls, while his servants wait outside of my door to escort me to this humiliation. My entire core trembles in fear of what the next moments hold.

There will be a thin line between my actions and their reactions. Accepting the fact that I may be seen as defiant but being secure in maintaining the integrity of my character no matter the response, is a choice that will dictate who I am for the rest of my life. I must choose to either submit to something that I do not agree with, or chew on all of the controversy that will be ridiculed against my convictions.

I brace myself behind the contemplation that has me frozen in time, and finally blurt out a resounding, NO!!

No, I will not be a victim of this outrage. No, I will not suffer this embarrassment for your pleasure! I will not be disgraced beyond recovery! No. I refuse. BUT AT WHAT COST? Controversy? No, disdain and brutal retaliation! I was pushed away from my security due to their distorted proclivities. Each wife fears now because of my determination to guard and protect my God given integrity. They do not support me, but cringe at the thought of a similar destiny.

The result; voices that have been quenched and relinquished from being free. Left silenced, dictated a similar fate, if they ever attempt to speak.

I now stand alone. Left without privilege, and open to the ridicule of every vile accusation that these same evil men have decided to attach to my name. Banned from existence like a criminal.

As if banning me from the palace was not enough, these accusers sought to ruin my reputation in such a way that it would be impossible for me to recover. Despite the fact that after his sobering, my king had second thoughts, his own fear and inability to stand against their tyranny, has allowed these advisors who desire to be cruel, and to create such fear, to make sure that no other woman in the kingdom would ever resist any of their demands again.

They say that I did not comply to their requests because my desire for admiration could only be gratified by other women. They tainted my love to be equal to their own by accusations of lewd practices that could not be satisfied by the admiration of men. What humiliation in response to such lascivious requests.

They say that my only desire was to liberate women into retaliation. But that is not true. My desire was to exercise my right of choice.

As painful as these tongue lashings were, they do not compare to the empty abandonment I have been doomed to live out for the rest of my life.

Not only was I banned from the king's presence, I was replaced! Replaced by a beautiful virgin princess whose fate also seemed to be exposed to these evil men. However, her protection rested in the hands of the great Jehovah God, who she would represent.

Lost and rejected, with the fear of deadly assassination looming over my head if I did not submit, I have made a conscious decision to stand up for what I believe. It is so humiliating to have to absorb the fact that the desires of men can be played out and upheld with absolutely no regard for those they victimize. These events have left the world to be afforded the privilege of judging who I am and what I am without ever entering my presence.

Can these privileges ever be justified or rationalized? THEY HAVE SEALED MY FATE. I am Vashti, Queen of Shushan. I refused to bow to the degradation of those who held my fate in their hands!! I SPEAK, so that my voice will hush the untruths of my demise and be a beacon of courage so that every woman will stand and persevere throughout the ages. They may have taken my crown, but they will not have my integrity or my soul.

# VOICE # 7

## *The Legion Voice*

Legion: 'The echo of many voices'

Have years of the female experience left women with a schizophrenic nature? Have our experiences caused us to live out life with split personalities that make us respond according to who we encounter?

The voice you are about to experience is one of multiple personalities. She is the compilation of many women that I have encountered throughout my life. The echoes of the bleating sounds of this Sisterhood are ringing in my ears as I pray. The tears of their pain long to clang a warning to the little Sisters who follow them. Their stories were buried, but they deserve to be acknowledged. I apologize if their stories are harsh. But this, my Sisters, is not a fairytale. It is not designed to offend them, but to free them. They have suffered, often alone, without resolve or care. Too afraid to divulge their script, they endured until the final act, sleeping with their scars.

Identifying with portions of this voice, may seem that I have entered into your personal space. However, this is simply a reminder that abuse knows no new stories, only a repetition of itself. You may be absorbing your personal sound in the echo of another. In fairness to their legacies, I say, "no more". So, without revealing their names and by camouflaging as much as possible, I give these forgotten women an extremely merited voice.

She sits crouched in a corner trying to drown out the laughter of the on lookers striving to hold the camera still as he stands with the two by four board striking her leg repeatedly. She cannot move because if she does, his erratic strikes may slip and hit her head. So, she must be still for her life. Besides, she is too afraid to be locked in that closet for days again, enduring his punishment.

CRAWL!

His kick knocked me back across the room,

CRAWL!

My tears are camouflaged by the blood that covers my lids.

Dear God, how long will he do this?

I am so tired.

Here we are again in this familiarity of humiliation. I hate to be in public. Each time I face my critics, I can feel the accusation of every stare as if I have misbehaved. Me, not him. I sit here with these huge, dark, glasses on as if they will assist in my deception, while he stands in front of the congregation, mesmerizing everyone, reputation seemingly intact, and I alone bear the burden of our secrets. I wanted to just stay home, but he treated it as sin. He seems to wear all of this self-assigned power like a badge of his manhood; his control.

It must be my fault! Look at me as I carry his eighteenth child. I hear the whispers. She must love him. She stays. They are obviously always in bed. I ask, is it love, or is it rape? Does anyone care? Stop talking and see my pain.

He is as cruel to them as he is to me. Twelve are gone. Released to better homes. While you surrendered to temptation, you allowed your taste to be tainted by the one who walked the streets. Even our grown sons knew her reputation. But you were so caught in her web that you wanted to throw me and our children from our home and give her everything that was rightfully mine. Your cruel beatings knocked our child's hand from my womb. I nearly died as the doctor laid me on our table and shoved my child back to safety. But despite my pain, I needed to check on our son at school. So, without hesitation, I went, still bearing the wardrobe of your brutality. The terror in his young eyes as he noticed the blood trickling down my legs will haunt us both forever.

You would think that the shock of punishment would bring change, but here I am with six more to protect. Year after year, twenty years of marriage, almost one per year and yet they stood in awe as the one who misbehaved had driven me to such a state that I threw him down a flight of stairs. I did not want to hurt him, I just needed to breathe, to stop the noise for just a moment so that I could regroup.

I have been suffocating for so long that what I love has become frustration to my nerves. I just needed a moment. I just needed a little help. But you avoided me, in public, like I carried the plague. So, at that moment, when I could not get my child to listen, I saw a flash of red and the next thing I knew everyone was screaming at me. Screaming, instead of helping.

I acknowledge my error, but will someone please see that I am drowning. If you won't help me, please, please save my children whose innocence deserves better.

There have been so many things that seem to be leading me to a path of no return. I have absolutely no say in anything! Shut up! He screams in my face. You are just a woman! He literally brought home wild animals for me to nurse to health. I am terrified. But he allows them to run around our home with more freedom than me. I am afraid to fall asleep. They tread the furniture with entitlement, climbing and scratching at me, while his stares dare me to complain. Leave? How? He made sure that I was so locked into his lifestyle that it is impossible to escape.

In the beginning I felt sheltered by the agenda of being taken care of. His knight in shining armor routine really worked on me. A woman needing to feel special. He could only see me, I stood out from all others. I felt the strength of what I thought was love. Even after two or three children his love seemed to remain strong. It was not until one comment, shortly after the birth of our third child, concerning ten extra pounds, that everything changed. It had only been five days. It seemed as if the light in his eyes dimmed as I slipped into a deep postpartum depression.

It didn't take long for me to understand that the fairy tale was not free. It came with stipulations and requirements that caused me to eventually lose sight of any form of protection or care.

Everything that we shared slipped away. I needed his permission to acquire even the most personal things. His humiliation grew as he found all sorts of ways to keep everything that he had out of my possession. If I expressed a need, he decided brand, amount, and distribution. Food became a luxury that only his taste received gratification for. It is a surprise that I know what a dollar even looks like. Hiding money from me became his greatest sport. I have wept sorely yet laughed slightly at the creative productivity of his game of hide and seek. Yes, the price is great, but now I am so invested, that it would be like an escape from Alcatraz to change it.

Many years ago, he decided that it would be better for me to leave our home. He said that I could be someone else's headache. So, for six months, we were apart. The day he arrived to 'take me home', he thought he was doing some sort of intervention that benefited me. In this false demonstration, I cannot help but quietly contemplate, this separation was the happiest I have been in years. Needless to say, he won, and I returned. One week later, I felt I had never left.

So, back on familiar ground, I dug in with all of myself, with everything that I thought would make him fall in love again. But the more I wore down, the more repulsive he viewed me. Every time things went wrong it somehow became my fault. I cut the grass, I hauled the wood, I treated him like a king with nothing to show for it except a sore back and an allergenic infection. You were the love of my life, yet you left me to be devoured by the wolves. Where were you when that alpha wolf sniffed out my existence? You left me without protection while he and his pack destroyed every ounce of my being. And you, you wore your glory as if you were a saint, while I bore the insult of a community that screamed error instead of seeing rejection. You left us!! Me, and your children! No food, no money, nothing! But the main thing you left me without was choice. I had no choice but to survive my plight until you decided that it was enough. You left us without your love and especially your protection. You chased wild affairs for years, leaving me to try to hide the shame of the poverty I was left with. When I searched for some inkling of care, I looked into deceptive eyes that only sought to further abuse me, to my shame, while your only response was accusation answered with more buffering of your ego.

I will bear those scars of question forever. Yet, I have protected your honor with my silence. And in return, not a thank you, not a back or foot rub, not even a sympathetic glance. It confused me when you decided that you were too sick to work and took a six-month sick leave from your already minimal job, without pay. But I worked hard to maintain our finances and keep us afloat while you screamed out your demands every day.

I had major surgery and as soon as I returned from the hospital, I needed to clean the house, cook supper, and prepare to satisfy every physical desire to your delight. The doctor demanded bed rest, but I lay awake nightly, too exhausted to sleep, with a hardness resting in my center core. I never get a day off. There are always children in the bed. Little feet are my facial message. Just when the pillow is right, there are cries whose frequency seem to only be tuned to the channels of my ears, amidst the violent suspirations in the air. Call me insane, but these facts have now become my reason for existence. My only complaint, I did not arrive at this place alone, yet I feel helpless to retaliate, and sentenced to stay.

I must have been crazy to want the 'bad boy'. The one whose attention you had to actually compete for. I thought I had arrived by becoming 'the one', 'the girl, 'the choice'. I was the nice girl. The one that others laughed at because she was too naïve to understand his betrayal. He was so cute and suave, and the monster did not reveal his teeth until I was already in his trap. "You are so skinny and shapeless. Why can't you be like your sister? You need to gain some weight." But thank you God for making me at least understand that this observation was simply an attempt to make me undesirable to every other man and seal my fate as his property. The only thing, I did not leave. The church made me feel as if I would be out of the will of God to break a vow. So, I endured the abuse for much too long.

I recently encountered an old friend. A good man who once thought I was phenomenal. At the time I knew him, he seemed too nerdy and disconnected for anyone to notice. So, I ignored him with disdain. But he got the girl that did not need to be popular. He loves her unconditionally and without reservation. His daily goal is to make her feel like a queen. No pretense, no hypocrisy, just a friendship and love that grows deeper every day. She only has to think it and he desires to fulfill it. They pray together, parent together, share every aspect of their lives and everything that he is, is hers to embrace and enjoy. Thank God for the heroes, the men who appreciate the gift that God gave when He created the woman. He is not afraid to be the symbol of kindness and love to his wife even though other men around him say he is weak. Many females miss the best while being mesmerized by the worse.

Living in a dysfunctional existence can make you forget that not all men view women as possessions to be handled like a subservient being. They know that she was created to complete him and together they are capable of conquering all limits.

He insulted me and slapped my face when my friend spoke to me after twenty years. There was nothing perverse or disrespectful about the salutation. It was a simple hello in my husband's presence. Just a kind gesture to a woman who seemed so disconnected from everyone and everything in the room. My husband's words of retaliation for this kindness both amused him, and he felt justified his misquote of scripture. *"If he had not plowed with my heifer, you would not have found out."* Found out what? "That I own you." Own me? This utterance is beyond comprehension! I am not yours to own.

The investment of time that is required to mistreat and abuse must be carried out by an individual with no love at all. When the abuser finally tires of all that it requires, they morph into a different form of abuse that exhibits no response at all. Viewed as insignificant already for years, his now incapable body scoots about as if he lives alone. She must assume what he thinks, what he feels, what he wants, and pray that she does not upset his system. She is so deep in his psyche that even the thought of the freedom of his demise causes her grief that she cannot control. To lose him would create a depression that would be hers as well. Her sealed fate, her final chain.

Abuse is bondage, but a lifetime of its personality and control is a prison that refuses to allow release. Defective relationships are manifested in such an obscure manner, that their release may disclose in many ways. Some women respond with the same hatred and attacks dished out to them. Others recoil and simply exist. Still others wait and pray for a rescue that will someday set them free.

Each of these may reap repercussions. The fighter eventually gets in a quarrel they cannot win, the frightened give their power away, and the dreamer must face annihilation before they see victory.

We, who are many, speak from our hurt, fear, and pain to every generation that will follow. Whose stories mimic the horrors of this voice. Our demise shall be your courage for change. We speak the truths of our experience, not to simply give abuse an audience, but to unmute the silence, and release the echoes that have a right to reverb throughout our history. THERE IS POWER IN OUR VOICE!! This sealed power MUST be heard!

So, what is the solution? How does the modern woman learn to cope with a society that seems to never change? We first choose to lean on the strength that our Mothers and Grandmothers, our Sisters and Friends, have shown us through the generations. Their love did not waver. Their tenacity endured the worse of situations. I am not suggesting that we just 'lay down and take it', but they taught us to understand that the evil dished out did not always have to be met with retaliation. They looked for something better and learned to love these dysfunctional men despite the abuse they dished out.

Secondly, we acknowledge that today, is a new day. An abundant life shift. It is a time to understand that there must be an awakening. That, my Sisters, is REAL Beauty! Beauty that cannot be purchased at the nearest cosmetic counter. It is real love. Love that refuses the bitterness of abuse to dictate our lives or happiness. It is what we are often too afraid to face. It is the power to walk away and repossess our dignity. God does not justify nor require that we live in fear or pain, PERIOD!!!

Some may wonder how God observes these things and does not zap them out of existence. How He seems to allow men to continue to get by and often do so in the name of being, the boss, the head, the one in charge.

He does not force any of us into good behavior but remember every action will reap a recompense of reward, good or evil. In that day of reckoning, He will change everything to the way it is supposed to be.

*And God shall wipe away all tears from their eyes; and there shall be no more death, neither sorrow, nor crying, neither shall there be any more pain; for the former things are passed away. (Revelation 21:4 KJV)*

And so, SHE lifts her voice and allows her echo to vibrate the atmosphere: She speaks for them all, so that they will be given the satisfaction of knowing someone cared enough to acknowledge her plight. She speaks so that her silent rest will not suggest that she lived in vain. She speaks so that the knowledge of her beauty reveals much more than her persona. It echoes and confesses her essence, as it unfolds the female experience.

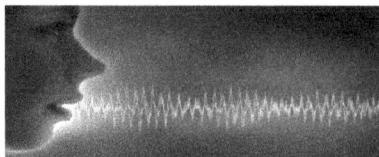

# FINALE

## *"I Have Survived the Storms"*

Whether I was coddled or neglected in my nativity really doesn't matter much.

Whether I was welcomed as a treasure or dismissed as a mistake, you have no right to determine my end. Your disdain may have temporarily placed me on shaky ground, but I refuse to allow it to plant me eternally.

Let me make you feel better and apologize for all of the trauma you think my arrival caused. But whether you solicited it or not, I was purposed to be here, to make my mark, to write my story.

And with every day, I rise to the occasion of my victory. I change the narrative of every gainsayer who felt they knew my end. I defy the odds against me, and I dare to reach for the stars!

His plans for me are my truth. I am no longer afraid to accept me. I am empowered by the love I both give and receive.
I hold my head so high that the atmosphere has to work overtime to accommodate my breathing.

The secret of my laughter is paralyzing to my face as it cradles my smile. I AM A WOMAN. I SHINE. I am exploding in the delight of the knowledge of this new information. I Am as free as I believe. I Am as beautiful as everything I choose to absorb. My echo is real. Its' reverb is singing a new song. It is reminding me, that the journey is mine to decide.

## **INFORMATION CONCERNING RUNAWAYS

I know that many times we are turned off, so to speak when statistics are presented to us. However, we must appreciate the time that many have put into keeping us informed. The story in Voice #4 is a true story that happened many years ago in the family of the Patriarch, Israel (Jacob). Even though the story is ancient, the details are still prevalent in modern society. We must keep our eyes open to the terror of those who abuse.

I have enclosed a recent list of facts that I feel will be helpful as we face the trials that plague our youth today. They still have a desire to 'get out'. They still want to be 'independent'. But now, more than ever, it is dangerous. What was once true for girls alone, has become true about all youths, no matter their gender. What is even more frightening, many times, they do not leave home at all. But the monsters are now lurking inside of our homes, in their bedrooms, and YOU probably purchased the source for their birthday or for Christmas!

The largest arena for solicitation of youths by predators is the internet. Please read and consider these facts:

*All statistical information provided has been gathered from*
***National Runaway Switchboard***

### *The Grooming Process*

Adolescence is a time of turmoil for many kids resulting in difficult relationships with parents as they are seeking to be independent adults. This is neither the fault of parents nor kids. Some kids may feel lonely, unsupported, that their parents are too strict, and that no one understands them. They may turn to the Internet and chat rooms to find someone they can talk to and feel a connection with. Unfortunately, this can be a recipe for disaster as predators wait for these vulnerable kids. Predators are master manipulators and provide the online "pretend" support these kids are looking for to build trust and to verify the child's feelings. They work at becoming that child's friend and gaining trust which is known as the grooming process. "It could continue for days or weeks before the pedophile begins bringing up sexual topics, *asking for explicit pictures* or for a *personal meeting*. By that time an emotional connection has been made."

After a nude picture is sent by the child, sometimes sextortion occurs; extortion using sexual images. This recently happened to a Massachusetts 13-year-old who thought *she was communicating with a teenager.* She sent him a naked photo. This man is *35* and from England. *He then threatened her* if she didn't send more naked pictures. Fortunately, this man is behind bars.

Another recent case involved a 12-year-old girl. A teacher happened to confiscate this girl's phone and noticed inappropriate text messages. The 28-year-old man from El Salvador was planning on *picking up this girl from school that afternoon.* The man had sent her the cellphone; *her mom didn't know she had one.*

These stories are alarming, and they are real. In both situations, these predators found their victim on Facebook.

Your teen comes home from school and goes up to his/her bedroom, closes the door and goes online. You worry who he or she may be talking to online. You are not alone. One of the biggest fears that parents have when kids go online is online predators, especially since more than 40 percent of kids have computers in their bedrooms with webcams.

The good news is that your child actually becoming the victim of an online predator is unlikely. The bad news is that according to FBI, "online predators are everywhere online," and are working hard to engage children online. Predators are not scary looking and do not stand out. They look like you or me or anyone down the street. They are "mostly male, although we are seeing an alarming trend of female predators. Male predators are often married with children. A professional, upstanding in the community but leading a deviant lifestyle through the Internet."

Parents need to pay attention to their children's online activity and take preventative measures to protect their children from online predators. No one wants their child to be that victim that we read about in the news all too frequently.

### How do predators connect with children online?

Chatrooms are a predators' dream come true and are the predominant online location where predators meet kids. Sites like *Omegle* that invite kids to talk to strangers are a parent's nightmare. Teaching your child not to talk to strangers is one of the first lessons in life that a parent gives their child. There are hundreds of these sites. Kids are naturally curious, and many kids visit them thinking it is no big deal. Kids should not be on these sites, *period.* They are disturbing and ripe with nudity and explicit disgusting sexual behavior in addition to being havens for predators.

Many *gaming sites* also have chatroom capabilities leaving a child vulnerable to potential exploitation. Many of these sites have webcam functionality. *"There are ways to turn the webcam on without you knowing you're being watched,"* said an FBI Special Agent.

Predators can also find kids on Facebook and other social networking sites. They often create a fake identity online and may *pose as a teenager*, the child never the wiser. Many kids become friends with complete strangers online with 70 percent of kids accepting "friend" requests regardless of whether they know who they are friending. A little less than half (43 percent) of teenagers who first met someone online later *met them in real life.*

YouTube and other video sites where kids post videos about themselves is another vehicle for predators to find children. *The more information kids post about themselves online the easier it is for a predator to find them.* Pictures of kids in school sports uniforms, talking about their school or activity, posting where they are on their status updates, or using Foursquare a geo-location site.

There are many opportunities for predators to compile the puzzle pieces to find out more about a child, their tastes in music, TV, and ultimately where they're located. Many kids are indiscriminate about the information they are posting online, on their social networking profiles for the world to see.

According to a *Harris interactive/McAffee study,* more than half of teens (52 percent) have given out personal information online to someone they don't know offline including personal photos and/or physical descriptions of themselves. Many 13- to 17-year-olds (69 percent) have updated their status on social networking sites to include their physical location, 28 percent chatted with strangers (people whom they did not know in the offline world) and 12 percent have posted their cellphone number.

### *Statistics Parents Should Know*

- More than 500,000 **predators** are online everyday
- Kids 12 to 15 are susceptible to being **groomed and manipulated** by offenders online
- FBI stats show that more than **50 percent of victims** of online sexual exploitation are 12-15 years old
- 89 percent of all sexual advances toward our children take place in **internet chat rooms** and through instant messaging.
- In (27 percent) of exploitation incidents, predators **asked kids for sexual photographs** of themselves.
- 4 percent of kids get "aggressive" sexual solicitations that included **attempts to contact the kids offline.**

### *What Can Parents Do?*

1. Self-education- Learn what kids may be exposed to online – Learn what the risks are.

2. Communicating, educating, e-mentoring your kids about:

- Online risks
- Chatrooms, game site risks
- Predators and to be aware of manipulative behavior, gifts, requests for nude pictures, grooming.
- Predators don't look scary, they look like you or I, or the person down the street.
- Teaching your child that if they get in a situation that feels uncomfortable, that they should and can always come to you and that they won't get in trouble if they do.
- Only friend people they know on Social Networking Sites
- Never meet someone they've met online without talking to an adult first.
- Turn off webcam when not in use

3. E-mentor kids online especially when they have a computer in their bedroom. Screen Retriever enables parents to monitor children's computer activity live wherever the child's computer is located in the home including who your child is communicating with using their webcam.

4. Set limits and ground rules about what your child is allowed to do online, sites they visit, information they post, who their friends are on social networking sites, who they are chatting with. Go over the Screen Retriever tips before they are allowed on the computer.

5. Learn the language your kids use on the computer and cellphone, like A/S/L or GNOC.

6. When your child comes to you with a problem, be there for them, and don't overreact. Many kids don't tell their parents when they have a problem online because they are afraid, they will lose computer privileges.

7. Start e-mentoring early when kids go on the computer so that your family values and rules are ingrained early.

One child caught in the manipulative trap of a predator is one too many. This can be prevented when parents "parent online" and "e-mentor".

This article is by PATCH Health & Fitness. Statistics about *Online Predators and Precautions Parents Should Take* contributed by a community member: Victoria Kempf / Safety Blogger March 12. 2012.

### *The National Runaway Switchboard*

No teenager ever aspires to become homeless, running from the very people who were supposed to care and protect him. However, 1.6 to 2.8 million teens run away from home each year, according to the National Runaway Switchboard. Many of these teenagers are abused sexually, physically and emotionally. They run for safety but instead end up fleeing right into an abyss of dangerous predators seeking vulnerable youth who only yearn for the comfort of a caring body.

### *Causes for Running Away from Home*

- 47% of teen runaways reported that they were having a conflict with a parent or guardian.

- Approximately 50% of teens reported that their parents kicked them out of the house or didn't care that they left.

- 80% of youth reported sexual or physical abuse before running away.

### *Depression*

Teenagers who become depressed may have a difficult time with decision making and may act on impulse. Since the *depressed teen* may not understand the emotions and thoughts running through him, he may blame his parents for his problems. This then leads to the false realization that being away from them will solve all of their issues.

### Oppositional defiant disorder

Another mental disorder that many teen runaways suffer from is oppositional defiant disorder, also called conduct disorder. They have a difficult time obeying authority and will act out in retaliation to anyone who tries to tell them what to do. Their actions are impulsive and can sometimes be threatening. They run away because they don't want to follow anyone's rules besides their own.

### Substance Abuse

According to the website, **TroubledTeenSearch.com,** 71% of surveyed street youths in Los Angeles abused drugs and/or alcohol. These substances act on the mind very much like mental illness, leading to impulsivity and poor judgment skills. Not only does this lead many teenagers to run away, but it also propels them into a life of drugs, alcohol, crime and abuse on the streets.

### *Difficulties in Adolescence*

Adolescents have a difficult time expressing their thoughts and emotions at times. This can cause them to feel powerless. To gain back that control, they feel as though they need to break away from the chains of parents and authority. They feel that if they can make it on their own, they will be able to show everyone how much they really know.

Adolescents who run away from home are usually running away from something they can't face. This could be parental separation, sexual orientation, bullying in school and other traumatic events. Teenagers don't runaway for attention but to escape the realities of a world they are afraid of or exhausted from living in. They want to be free from the devastation and find a new happiness.

### *Life on the Streets*

Most runaways return home within 48 hours to a week and will typically stay with friends, according to the National Runaway Switchboard. However, the longer teenagers stay away from home, the higher the risk they have of becoming victims of perpetrators (abuse and assault). Involvement in gangs, illegal activities, and suicide are all possible results of homelessness.

### *Teen Runaway Help*

If you are a runaway, you don't have to run anymore. You can get help. Call 1-800-RUNAWAY. They have people who will help you find shelters and the assistance you need to make it back on the right path, even if that isn't home for you.

If you do want to go home but have no idea how to get there from where you are or just don't have the money, National Runaway Switchboard has a program that will help you get home on Greyhound bus lines free. Simply call their number for help.

### *Parent Tips for Dealing with a Runaway Situation*

If you suspect your teenager has run away, follow these steps:

- Call his friends to ask about the last time they saw him.
- Visit local hangouts or possible places he may have gone.
- Check her room and belongings to find any clues of her whereabouts.
- Call the police to report a missing person.

- Acquire caller ID in case your teenager calls.

- Call area shelters to check to see if he has contacted them and ask for further information on who to call.

- Call *1-800-RUNAWAY* for even more information on your plan of action.

- Check out the ***Help Find My Child*** website for support and further assistance in your search.

### *If Your Teen Calls*

Remain as calm as possible if your teenager calls. Show that you are genuinely concerned and care for her. Urge her to come home but listen as well. Many teens just want the chance to be heard. Refrain from saying anything negative to your teen, for example, "When you get home, you're going to be grounded." Take this running away as a serious sign that something is wrong and that your son or daughter needs help.

### *When Your Teen Comes Home*

It's a very emotional and sensitive time when a runaway comes home. He feels apprehensive about walking in the door because he doesn't know what to expect. Understand that this was as traumatic for him as it has been for you. Take this time to show your teenager that you are willing to work through any of the difficulties he is having and that you accept his return with open arms. The following are some other tips:

- Listen to your teen and take down any help that he may need since his absence such as medical attention and/or counseling.

- Call all the people you contacted about his disappearance to let them know he is home.

- Make a conscious effort to show how appreciative you are to have him home, that you love him and want to care for him as he wants to be cared for.

- If your teenager is defiant, contact your local help line.

*These issues are at an epidemic state. I encourage you to be careful and attentive to things that occur both in and around your home. If you need help, don't be afraid to ask.*

*The Author*

www.ingramcontent.com/pod-product-compliance
Lightning Source LLC
Chambersburg PA
CBHW021239090426
42740CB00006B/609